William Sherlock

The Case of Resistance of the Supreme Powers Stated and Resolved

William Sherlock

The Case of Resistance of the Supreme Powers Stated and Resolved

ISBN/EAN: 9783337814069

Printed in Europe, USA, Canada, Australia, Japan

Cover: Foto ©Lupo / pixelio.de

More available books at **www.hansebooks.com**

THE CASE OF Resistance

OF THE
SUPREME POWERS
Stated and Resolved,

According to the

DOCTRINE

OF THE
Holy Scriptures.

By *WILL. SHERLOCK*, D.D.
Rector of St. *George Buttolph-lane*, *London*.

LONDON: Printed for *Fincham Gardiner*,
at the *White-horse* in *Ludgate-street*. 1684.

TO THE
Right Honourable
FRANCIS
Lord *GUILFORD*,

Lord Keeper of the
Great Seal of *ENGLAND*,
and one of
His Majesties most Honourable
PRIVY COUNCIL.

My Lord,

I Humbly beg leave to present to your Lordships hands, a very plain Discourse, but very necessary in such an
Age

The Dedication.

Age as this, wherein the principles of Rebellion are openly profest and taught, and the Doctrine of Non-resistance and Passive Obedience, not confuted, but laught out of countenance.

There have been indeed a great many excellent Books writ upon this Argument by learned men; but I fear most of them are too learned for ordinary Readers, who most need instruction, and are most easily poisoned with Seditious Doctrines; and therefore there is still occasion enough for such a small Treatise as this, which I hope is fitted to the understanding of the meanest men, who will be so honest, as impartially to consider it: and those who will not read nor consider, what is offered for their conviction, are out of the reach

The Dedication.

reach of all instruction, and must be governed by other methods.

My Lord,

Your Lordships known Loyalty and Zeal for the service of the Crown, which by the favour of a wise and discerning Prince has deservedly advanced you to so high a Station, made me presume, that such a present as this, though in it self very mean, might not be unacceptable to you, especially when it is intended as a publick acknowledgment (the best which my mean circumstances in the World enable me to make) of those great favours I have received from your Lordship.

That God would bless your Lordship with a long Life, and vigorous Age, and encrease of Honour,

The Dedication.

nour, for the service of the King, and of the Church, is the prayer of,

My Lord,

Your Lordships
most humble and
most obedient Servant,

W. SHERLOCK.

THE CASE OF Resistance

OF THE

SUPREME POWERS

Stated and Resolved,

According to the Doctrine of the Holy SCRIPTURES.

The INTRODUCTION.

I Presume, I need make no apologie for the seasonableness of this Discourse at this time: for if ever it be fit to put People in mind of that Subjection which they owe to the Higher Powers, no time can be more proper for it, than when we see the Peace and Security of

The Introduction.

Publick Government disturbed and endangered by *Popish* and *Fanatick Conspiracies*, who like *Sampson's Foxes*, though they look very different ways, yet are tyed together by the *Tail* with a *Firebrand* between them; and had not the good Providence of God wonderfully appeared for the preservation of his *Anointed*, I am sure it had been a very unseasonable time now to have treated on this Subject: and therefore, setting aside all *Apologies*, I shall onely give a brief account of the designe of this following *Treatise*.

There are three ways of proving and confirming the *Doctrine* of *Non-resistance*, or *Subjection* to *Soveraign Princes*. 1. By the *Testimonies* of the *Holy Scriptures*. 2. By the Doctrine and Practice of the Primitive Christians. 3. By the fundamental Constitutions of that particular Government under which we live. I have considered the last, as much as was necessary to my purpose. The second I have not meddled with: for whoever has a mind to be satisfied about it, may consult that admirable Discourse of *Archbishop Usher*, about the Power of the *Prince*, and the Obedience of the *Subject*; which will not cost much money, nor take

The Introduction.

take up much time to read it. But the designe I proposed to my self, was carefully to consider the Testimonies of Scripture, which are beyond all other Authorities, and to vindicate them from the Cavils and Exceptions of the several Patrons of *Resistance*. And the whole Discourse is divided into these following Chapters.

1. The First contains the Authorities of the *Old Testament*; wherein I have plainly shewn, that *God* himself set up a Soveraign and Irresistible Power in the *Jewish Nation*; and that during all that time, it was unlawful for *Subjects*, upon any pretence whatsoever, to resist *their Princes*.

2. The Second contains the Doctrine of our *Saviour*, concerning Subjection to *Soveraign Princes*.

3. The Third contains an account of our *Saviour*'s Example in this matter.

4. The Fourth considers what Saint *Paul*'s Doctrine was about Subjection.

5. The Fifth, the Doctrine of Saint *Peter*.

6. The Sixth contains an Answer to the most popular Objections against *Non-resistance*.

In examining the Authorities of *Scri-*

pture, I have carefully considered whatever has been plausibly urged in defence of the *Doctrine* of *Resistance*, and reduced it under those particular *Texts* which have been thought most to favour it: and I do not know of any thing material, which has been pleaded in this Cause, which I have wholly omitted. Possibly some may complain, that I have not observed the exact *Rules* of *Art* and *Method* in this, to propose the *Question*, to explain the *Terms* of it, to produce my *Proofs*, and then to answer the *Objections* which are made against it. Now this I must acknowledge in part to be true; and I think this *Discourse* never the less perfect for that. The Proposition I undertake to prove, is this: That *Soveraign Princes*, or the *Supreme Power* in any Nation, in whomsoever it is plac'd, is in all cases irresistible. This is a plain Proposition, which needs no explanation: and the way I take to prove it, is as plain; by producing the *Testimonies* of *Scripture* both of the *Old* and *New Testament*, as they lie in order, and shewing what *Power* they grant to *Princes*, and what *Obedience* they require of *Subjects*. This is the fairest way I could think on, to give my *Readers* a full view

of

of the *Doctrine* of the *Scriptures* in this matter; and this was all I intended to do: for I am verily perswaded, that were men once convinced that *Resistance* of *Princes* is expresly contrary to the *Doctrine* both of the *Old* and *New Testament*, it would be no easie matter, by any other Arts or Pretences, to draw the most fanatical and factious persons amongst us (who retain any Reverence for God) into a Rebellion.

CHAP. I.

Wherein the Unlawfulness of Resisting the Supreme Powers is proved, from the Authority of the Old Testament.

TO prove the unlawfulness of *Resistance*, I shall begin with the Old Testament. Now there is nothing more evident, than that God set up such a Supreme and Soveraign Power in the *Jewish Nation*, as could not, and ought not to be resisted by the Fundamental Laws of their Government. For this is all I am concerned at present to prove, That it is never lawful to resist the *Higher Powers*; not that the Supreme and Soveraign power is always to be *in a single Person*, but that wherever it is, it is irresistible, and that whenever this Supreme power by the *Laws* of the *Nation*, is invested in a *single Person*, such a Prince must not upon any pretence whatsoever be resisted.

The first Governour God set over the Chil-

Children of *Israel*, when he brought them out of the Land of *Egypt*, was *Moses*; and I think I need not prove how Sacred and irresistible his Authority was. This is sufficiently evident in the rebellion of *Korah, Dathan,* and *Abiram*, against *Moses* and *Aaron*, when God caused the earth to open her mouth and swallow them up, 16 *Numbers*. And lest this should be thought an extraordinary case, *Moses* and *Aaron* being extraordinary persons, immediately appointed by God, and governed by his immediate direction; the Apostle St. *Jude* alleadges this example against those in his days, who were turbulent and factious, *who despised dominions, and spake evil of dignities, that they should perish in the gainsaying of Core*, *Jud. v.* 11. which he could not have done, had not this example extended to all ordinary, as well as extraordinary Cases; had it not been a lasting testimony of Gods displeasure against all those, who oppose themselves against the *Soveraign powers.* But *Moses* was not always to rule over them, and therefore God expresly provides for a Succession of *Soveraign power*, to which they must all submit. The *ordinary Sovereign* power of the *Jewish*

Nation after *Moses* his death, was devolved either on the *high Priest*, or those extraordinary persons whom God was pleased to raise up, such as *Joshua* and the several *Judges*, till in *Samuels* days it setled in their *Kings*. For as for the *Jewish Sanhedrim*, whose power is so much extolled by the *Jewish Writers*, who are all of a late date, many years since the destruction of *Jerusalem*, and therefore no competent *witnesses* of what was done so many ages before, it does not appear from any testimony of Scripture, that there was any such *Court* of *Judicature*, till after their return from the *Babylonish Captivity*.

But yet God took care to secure the Peace and good Government of the Nation, by appointing such a power as should receive the last *Appeals*, and whose *Sentence* in all *Controversies* should be final, and uncontroulable, as you may see in the 17 *Deut.* 8, 9, 10, 11, 12 *v*. There were inferiour Magistrates and *Judges* appointed in their several Tribes and Cities, which *Moses* did by the advice of *Jethro* his Father-in-law, and by the approbation of God, *Exod.* 18. But as the Supreme Power was still reserved in the hands of *Moses*, while he he lived, so it is here secured to the *high Priest*, or *Judges*, after his death; for it is expresly appointed, that if those inferiour *Judges* could not determine the Controversie, they should come unto the *Priests*, *the Levites*, that is, the Priests of the *Tribe of Levi*, (who by the 12 *ver.* appears only to be the *High Priest*) *and to the Judge that shall be in those days*, that is, if it shall be at such a time, when there is an extraordinary Judge raised by God, (for there were not always such *Judges* in *Israel*, as is evident to any one who reads the Book of *Judges*) *and of them they should inquire, and they shall shew the sentence of Judgment*; and *thou shalt do according to the Sentence which they of that place*, (*which the Lord shall choose*) *shall shew thee, and thou shalt observe to do according to all they shall inform thee.* Where the Place which God shall choose, signifies the Place which he should appoint for the *Ark* of the *Covenant*, and for the *Levitical worship*; which was the place where the *high Priest*, and the *chief Judge* or Ruler of *Israel*, when there was any such person, had their ordinary residence; which was at first at *Shilo*, and afterwards at *Jerusalem*.

And

And what the Authority of the *chief Priest*, or of the *Judge* when there was one, was in those days, appears from *v.* 12. *And the man that will do presumptuously, and will not hearken to the Priest, (that standeth to minister there before the Lord thy God) or unto the Judge, even that man shall die, and thou shalt put away the evil from Israel.* This is as absolute Authority, as the most absolute *Monarch* in the world can challenge, that disobedience to their last and final determination, what ever the cause be, shall be punisht with death: and what place can there be for *Resistance* in such a Constitution of Government as this? It is said indeed in *v.* 11. according *to the sentence of the Law, which they shall teach thee, and according to the judgment that they shall tell thee, thou shalt do.* And hence some conclude, that they were not bound to abide by their sentence, nor were punishable, if they did not, but onely in such cases, when they gave sentence according to the Law of God. But these men do not consider that the matter in controversie is supposed to be doubtful, and such as could not be determined by the *inferiour Courts,* and therefore is submitted

ted to the decision of the *Supreme Judge*; and as he determined, so they must do; and no man, under the penalty of death, must presume to do otherwise: which takes away all liberty of judging from private persons, though this *Supreme Judge* might possibly mistake in his Judgment, as all *humane Judicatures* are liable to mistakes; but it seems God Almighty thought it necessary that there should be some final Judgment, from whence there should be no *appeal*, notwithstanding the possibility of a mistake in it.

So that there was a *Supreme* and *Soveraign*, that is, unaccountable and irresistible Power in the *Jewish Nation* appointed by God himself: for indeed it is not possible that the publick Peace and Security of any *Nation* should be preserved without it. And I think it is as plain, that when the *Jews* would have a *King*, their *Kings* were invested with this *Supreme* and *Irresistible Power*: for when they desired a *King*, they did not desire a meer *nominal* and *titular King*, but a *King to judge them*, and *to go out before them, and fight their battels*; that is, a *King* who had the Supreme and Soveraign Authority, 1 *Sam.* 8. 6. 19. 20.

a *King* who should have all that power of Government, excepting the peculiar acts of the Priestly Office, which either their *High-Priest* or their *Judges* had before.

And therefore when *Samuel* tells them what shall be the *manner* of their *King*, 11 *ver.* though what he says does necessarily suppose the translation of the Soveraign and Irresistible power to the person of their *King*, yet it does not suppose that the *King* had any new power given him more than what was exercised formerly by their *Priests* and *Judges*. He does not deter them from chusing a *King*, because a *King* should have greater power, and be more uncontroulable and irresistible than their other *Rulers* were: for *Samuel* himself had had as soveraign and irresistible a power as any King, being the Supreme Judge in *Israel*, whose Sentence no man could disobey or contradict, but he incurred the penalty of death, according to the Mosaical Law. But the reason why he disswades them from chusing a *King*, was because the external *Pomp* and *Magnificence* of *Kings* was like to be very chargeable and oppressive to them. *He will take your sons and appoint them for himself,*

himself, for his chariots, and to be his horsemen, and some shall run before his chariots. And he will appoint him captains over thousands, and captains over fifties, and will set them to ear his ground, and to reap his harvest. And thus in several particulars he acquaints them what burdens and exactions they will bring upon themselves by setting up a *King*, which they were then free from: and if any *Prince* should be excessive in such exactions, yet they had no way to help themselves; they must not resist nor rebel against him, nor expect, that what inconvenience they might find in *Kingly Government*, God would relieve and deliver them from it, when once they had chose a *King: Ye shall cry out in that day, because of your King which ye have chosen you, and the Lord will not hear you in that day, v.* 18. That is, God will not alter the *government* for you again, how much soever you may complain of it.

This, I say, is a plain proof that their *Kings* were invested with that Soveraign Power which must not be resisted, though they oppress their Subjects to maintain their own State, and the Grandeur and Magnificence of their Kingdom.

dom. But I cannot think, that these words contain the *original grant* and Charter of Regal power, but only the translation of that power which was formerly in their *high-Priests* or *Judges to Kings*. *Kings* had no more power than their other Governours had: for there can be no power greater than that which is irresistible; but this power in the hands of *Kings* was likely to be more burdensome and oppressive to them, than it was in the hands of their *Priests* and *Judges*, by reason of their different way of living; which is the onely argument *Samuel* uses to dissuade them from transferring the *Supreme* and *Soveraign power* to *Princes*. And therefore I rather choose to Translate *Mishpat*, as our Translators do, *by the manner of the King*, than as other learned men do, *by the right of the King*, thereby understanding the original Charter of Kingly power: for it is not the Regal power which *Samuel* here blames, which is no other but the very same power which he himself had, while he was Supreme *Judge* of *Israel*, but their pompous way of living, which would prove very oppressive and burdensome to them, and be apt to make them complain, who had not been used to such exactions. And

And here before I proceed, give me leave to make a short digression in vindication of *Kingly Government*, which some men think is greatly disparaged by this story. For 1. It is evident that God was angry with the *Jews* for desiring a *King*; and declared his anger against them, by sending a violent tempest of Thunder and Rain in Wheat-harvest; which made them confess, *that they had added to all their sins this evil, to ask a King*, 1 *Sam.* 12. 16, 17. &c. From whence some conclude, that Kingly power and Authority is so far from being the Original appointment and constitution of God, that it is displeasing to him. And 2. that *Samuel* in describing *the manner of the King*, represents it as oppressive and uneasie to Subjects, and much more burdensome, and less desirable than other Forms of Government.

1. As for the first, it must be acknowledged, that God was angry with the *Children of Israel* for asking a *King*: but then these men mistake the reason, which was not because God is an enemy to *Kingly Government*, but because he himself was the *King of Israel*; and by asking a *King* to go in and out before them, they exprest a dislike of *Gods Government*

The Case of Resistance of

ment of them. Thus God tells *Samuel, They have not rejected thee, but they have rejected me, that I should not reign over them,* 1 *Sam.* 8. 7. And thus *Samuel* aggravates their sin, *that they said, Nay but a King shall reign over us; when the Lord your God was your King,* 12 *Chap.* 12. *v.*

Now the Crime had been the same, had they set up an *Aristocratical* or *Democratical* Government, as well as *Regal* Power, in derogation of Gods Government of them. Their fault was not in choosing to be governed by a single person; for so they had been governed all along, by *Moses* and *Joshua,* by their *high Priests,* or those other extraordinary *Judges* whom God had raised up, and at this very time by *Samuel* himself; for it is a great mistake to think that the Jews, before they chose a *King,* were governed by a *Synedrial power,* like an *Aristocracy* or *Democracy,* which there is not the least appearance of in all the *Sacred History*; for as for those persons whom *Moses* by the advice of *Jethro* set over the people, they were not a supreme or *Soveraign Tribunal,* but such *Subordinate Magistrates* as every *Prince* makes use of for administring Justice to

the

the People. *They were Rulers of thousands, Rulers of hundreds, Rulers of fifties, Rulers of tens,* 18 *Exod.* 21. and were so far from being one standing Judicature, that they were divided among their several Tribes and Families; and were so far from being supreme, that *Moses* still reserved all difficult cases, and last appeals, that is, the true Soveraign power to himself, as it was afterwards by an express Law reserved to the *High Priests*, and *Judges* extraordinarily appointed: and there is so little appearance of this Soveraign Tribunal in *Samuels* days, that he himself went in Circuit every year, as our Judges now do, to *Bethel* and *Gilgal*, and *Mizpeh*, and *judged Israel,* 1 *Sam.*7.16.

But the fault of *Israel* in asking a *King* was this, that they preferred the government of a King, before the immediate government of God. For the understanding of which, it will be necessary to consider briefly, how Gods government of *Israel* differ'd from their government by *Kings*. For when they had chose a *King*, did God cease to be the King of *Israel?* was not their King Gods Minister and Vicegerent, as their Rulers and Judges were before? was not

not the King God's Anointed? and did he not receive the Laws and Rules of Government from him? yes, this is in some measure true, and yet the difference is very great.

While God was the King of *Israel*, though he appointed a Supreme visible Authority in the Nation, yet the exercise of this Authority was under the immediate direction and government of God. *Moses* and *Joshua* did not stir a step, nor attempt any thing without Gods order, no more than a menial servant does without the direction of his Master. In times of Peace, they were under the ordinary government of the *High Priest*, who was God's immediate servant, who declared the Law to them, and in difficult cases, referred the cause to God, who gave forth his answers by him: when they were opprest by their enemies, which God never permitted, but for their sins, when they repented and begged Gods pardon and deliverance, God raised up some *extraordinary persons* endued with an extraordinary spirit, to fight their Battels for them, and subdue their Enemies, and to judge *Israel*; and these men did every thing by a Divine impulse and inspiration, as *Moses* and

and *Joshua* did. So that they were as immediately governed by God, as any man governs his own house and Family. But when the Government was put into the hands of *Kings*, God in a great measure left the administration of it to the will and pleasure of *Princes*, and to the methods of humane Governments and Policy.

Though God did immediately appoint *Saul*, and afterwards *David* to be King, yet ordinarily the government descended not by God's immediate choice, but by the *right* of *Succession*: and though some Kings were Prophets too, yet it was not often so; they were not so immediately directed by God as the *Judges* of old were, but had their Councels of State for advice in peace and war, and their standing Armies and Guards for the defence of their Persons and Government. They were indeed commanded to govern by the Laws of *Moses*, to consult the Oracles of God in difficult cases, and God raised up extraordinary Prophets to direct them, but still it was in their own power, whether they would obey the Laws of God, or hearken to his Prophets; good Kings did, and bad Kings did not; and therefore

fore the government of *Israel* by Kings, was like other humane governments, lyable to all the defects and miscarriages which other governments are; whereas while the government was immediately in God's hands, they did not only receive their *Laws*, and external *Polity* from him, but the very executive power was in God: for though it was administred by Men, yet it was administred by God's immediate direction, with the most exact Wisdom, Justice and Goodness.

This was the sin of the *Jews*, that they preferred the Government of an earthly King, before having God for their King; and this must be acknowledged to be a great fault, but it is such a fault, as no other Nation was ever capable of, but only the *Jews*, because God never vouchsafed to be *King* of any other Nation in such a manner; and therefore we must not compare Kingly government, for there is no competition between them, with the Government of God, but we must compare Kingly government with any other form of humane Government; and then we have reason to believe, that notwithstanding God was angry with the *Jews*, and this was a case peculiar to the *Jews* for desiring

ring a *King*, that yet he prefers Kingly government before any other, because when he forefaw that the *Jews* would in time grow weary of his government, he makes provifion in their Law, for fetting up a King, not for fetting up an *Aristocratical* or *Democratical* power, which their Law makes no allowance for, as you may fee, 17 *Deuter*. 14.

2. Another objection againft Kingly power and Government, is, that *Samuel* in this place reprefents it as very oppreffive and burdenfome to the Subject. For what fome men anfwer, that *Samuel* fpeaks here only of the abufe of *Regal* Power, I think is not true; for the meer abufe of power is no Argument againft it, becaufe all kind and forms of power are lyable to be abufed, and by this reafon we fhould have no government at all. And it is evident, that *Samuel* does not mention any one thing here, that can be called an abufe of power, nothing but what is abfolutely neceffary to maintain the State and Magnificence of an *Imperial Crown*. For how can a Prince fubfift without Officers and Servants of all forts, both Men and Women, both for the ufes of his Family, and the fervice of his government both

in Peace and War? and how can this be maintained; but by a Revenue proportionable to the expence? and since none of them had such an estate, as to defray this charge themselves, whoever was to be chosen King, must have it from others, by publick Grants and publick Taxes, which he here expresses by *taking their fields and their vineyards, and their olive-yards, the tenth of their fields, and their vineyards, and the tenth of their sheep, for himself and his servants,* the tenth being the usual Tribute paid to the *Eastern Kings*. This is not an abuse of power, though some *Princes* might be excessive in all this, but it is *the manner of the King*, that which is necessary to his Royal State. There is nothing of all this forbid in 17 *Deuter.* where God gives Laws to the *King*; and indeed to forbid this, would be to forbid Kingly power, which cannot subsist without it.

Indeed I find some Learned men mistaken in this matter; for they take it for granted, that what *Samuel* here calls *the manner of the King*, is such an abuse of power, as God had expresly forbid to Kings in the 17 of *Deuter.* 16, 17. but why the abuse of Regal power should be be called *the manner* or *the right* of the King, is past my understanding. *Mishpat*, however you Translate it, must signifie something which is essential to Kingly government, otherwise *Samuels* Argument against chusing a *King* had been sophistical and fallacious. For there is no Form of Government but is lyable to great abuses, when it falls into ill hands: and this they had experience of at this very time; for the miscarriages of *Samuel's Sons*, was the great reason, why the people at this time desired a King, 1 *Sam.* 8. 3, 4, 5. And if we compare these two places together, what God forbids the King with what *Samuel* calls *the manner of the King*, we shall find nothing alike. In the 17 of *Deut.* 16, 17. v. God tells them, that their King *shall not multiply horses to himself, nor cause the people to return into Egypt, to the end that he should multiply horses, for as much as the Lord hath said unto you, Ye shall henceforth return no more that way.* God would not allow them to have any Commerce or intercourse with *Egypt*, and therefore forbid their *Kings* to multiply horses, with which *Egypt* did abound, that there might be no new familiarity contracted with that

Idolatrous Nation. Neither shall he *multiply wives to himself, that his heart turn not away.* Where *multiplying wives* seems plainly to refer to his taking wives of other Nations and other Religions, as appears from what is added, *that his heart turn not away:* that is, left they should seduce him to *Idolatry*, as we know *Solomon*'s wives did him, who are therefore said to *turn away his heart*, 1 *Kings* 11. 3, 4. *Neither shall he greatly multiply to himself silver and gold.* For such a covetous humour would mightily tempt him to oppress his Subjects. This is all that God expresly forbids their Kings, when they should have any. But now *Samuel* in describing *the manner of the King*, takes no notice of any thing of all this, but only tells them, that their *King* would appoint out fit persons for his service of their Sons and Daughters, that they should pay *Tribute* to him, and should themselves be his *servants*; not as servants signifies slaves and vassals, but Subjects, who owe all duty and service to their Prince as far as he needs them.

But what is it then that *Samuel* finds fault with in *Kingly power*, & which he uses as an argument to dissuade the Children

dren of *Israel* from desiring a King? why it is no more, than the necessary expences and services of *Kingly power*, which would be thought very grievous to them, who were a free people, and at that time subject to no publick services and exactions. The government they then lived under was no charge at all to them. They were governed, as I observed before, either by their *High Priest*, or by *Judges* extraordinarily raised by God. As for their *High Priests*, God himself had allotted their maintenance sutable to the quality and dignity of their Office; and therefore they were no more charge to the people when they were their Supreme Governors, than they were, when the power was in other hands, either in the hands of *Judges* or *Kings*. As for their *Judges* whom God raised up, they affected nothing of Royal greatness, they had no Servants or Retinue, standing Guards or Armies to maintain their Authority, which was secured by that Divine power with which they acted, not by the external pomp and splendour of a Court. Thus we find *Moses* appealing to God in the Rebellion of *Korah*, *I have not taken one Ass from them, neither have I hurt any of them,*

them, 16 *Numbers* 15. And thus *Samuel* appeals to the Children of *Israel* themselves, *Behold, here I am, witness against me before the Lord, and before his Anointed; whose Oxe have I taken? or whose Ass have I taken? or whom have I defrauded? whom have I oppressed? or of whose hands have I received any bribe to blind mine eyes therewith? and I will restore it*, 1 *Sam.* 12. 3. Now a people, who lived so free from all Tributes, exactions, and other services due to Princes, must needs be thought sick of ease and liberty, to exchange so cheap, so free a State, for the necessary burdens and expences of Royal power, though it were no more than what is necessary; which is the whole of *Samuels* argument, not that Kingly government is more expensive and burdensome than any other form of humane government, but that it was to bring a new burden upon themselves, when they had none before. No humane Governments, whether *Democracies* or *Aristocracies*, can subsist, but upon the publick charge; and the necessary expences of *Kingly power* are not greater than of a *Commonwealth*. I am sure this *Kingdom* did not find their burdens eased by pulling down their *King*; and

I believe, whoever acquaints himself with the several forms of government, will find *Kingly Power* to be as easie upon this score, as Commonwealths. So that what *Samuel* discourses here, and which some men think so great a reflection upon *Kingly government*, does not at all concern us, but was peculiar to the state and condition of the *Jews* at that time.

Let us then proceed to consider how sacred and irresistible the Persons and Authority of *Kings* were under the *Jewish Government*; and there cannot be a plainer example of this, than in the case of *David*. He was himself aneinted to be *King after Saul*'s death, but in the mean time was grievously persecuted by *Saul*, pursued from one place to another, with a designe to take away his life. How now does *David* behave himself in this extremity? What course does he take to secure himself from *Saul*? Why he takes the onely course that is left a Subject; he flies for it, and hides himself from *Saul* in the Mountains and Caves of the Wilderness; and when he found he was discovered in one place, he removes to another: He kept Spies upon *Saul* to observe his motions,

not

not that he might meet him to give him Battel, or to take him at an advantage; but that he might keep out of his way, and not fall unawares into his hands.

Well, but this was no thanks to *David*, becauſe he could do no otherwiſe. He was too weak for *Saul*, and not able to ſtand againſt him; and therefore had no other remedy but flight. But yet we muſt conſider, that *David* was a man of War, he ſlew *Goliah*, and fought the Battels of *Iſrael* with great ſucceſs; he was an admired and beloved Captain, which made *Saul* ſo jealous of him; the eyes of *Iſrael* were upon him for their next King, and how eaſily might he have raiſed a potent and formidable Rebellion againſt *Saul*! But he was ſo far from this, that he invites no man to his aſſiſtance; and when ſome came uninvited, he made no uſe of them in an offenſive or defenſive War againſt *Saul*. Nay, when God delivered *Saul* two ſeveral times into *David*'s hands, that he could as eaſily have killed him, as have *cut off the skirts of his garment at Engedi*, 1 Sam. 24. or as have taken that *ſpear away which ſtuck in the ground at his bolſter, as he did in the hill of Hachilah*, 1 Sam. 26. yet he would neither touch
Saul

Saul himself, nor suffer any of the people that were with him to do it, though they were very importunate with him for liberty to kill *Saul*; nay, though they urged him with an argument from Providence, that it was a plain evidence that it was the Will of God that he should kill *Saul*, because God had now delivered his enemy into his hands, according to the promise he had made to *David*, 1 *Sam.* 24. 4. 26 *ch. ver.* 8. We know what use some men have made of this argument of Providence, to justifie all the *Villanies* they had a mind to act: but *David*, it seems, did not think that an opportunity of doing evil, gave him licenſe and authority to do it. Opportunity, we say, makes a *Thief*, and it makes a *Rebel*, and it makes a *Murderer*: no man can do any Wickedness, which he has no opportunity of doing; and if the Providence of God, which puts such opportunities into mens hands, justifies the wickedness they commit, no man can be chargeable with any guilt whatever he does; and certainly opportunity will as soon justifie any other sin, as Rebellion and the Murder of Princes. We are to learn our duty from the Law of God, not from his Providence;

dence; at least, this must be a setled Principle, that the Providence of God will never justifie any action which his Law forbids.

And therefore, notwithstanding this opportunity which God had put into his hands to destroy his enemy, and to take the Crown for his reward, *David* considers his duty, remembers, that though *Saul* were his enemy, and that very unjustly, yet he was the *Lords Anointed*. *The Lord forbid*, says he, *that I should do this unto my Master the Lords Anointed, to stretch forth my hand against him, seeing he is the Lords Anointed*. Nay, he was so far from taking away his life, that his heart smote him for cutting off the skirt of his Garment. And we ought to observe the reason *David* gives, why he durst not hurt *Saul*, Because he was *the Lords Anointed*; which is the very reason the Apostle gives in the 13 *Rom.* 1, 2. *because the powers are ordained of God; and he that resisteth the power, resisteth the ordinance of God*. For to be anointed of God, signifies no more than that he was made King by God. Thus *Josephus* expounds being *anointed by God*, ὑπὸ τοῦ Θεοῦ βασιλεὺς ἀξιωθεὶς, one who had the Kingdom bestowed on him

God; and ὑπὸ τῦ Θεῦ κεχειροτονημένος, one who was ordained by God. For it seems by this phrase, he look'd upon the external ceremony of *Anointing* to be like imposition of hands, which in other cases consecrated Persons to peculiar offices. For this external Unction was onely a visible signe of Gods designation of them to such an office; and when that was plain, they were as much *God's Anointed* without this visible Unction as with it. *Cyrus* is called God's Anointed, though he never was anointed by any Prophet, but onely designed for his Kingdom by Prophesie, 45 *Isai*. 1. And we never read in Scripture, that any *Kings* had this external Unction, who succeeded in the Kingdom by right of inheritance, unless the Title and Succession were doubtful; and yet they were the Lord's Anointed too, that is, were plac'd in the Throne by him. So that this is an eternal reason against resisting Soveraign Princes, that they are set up by God, and invested with his authority; and therefore their Persons and their authority are sacred.

But yet there are some men, who from the example of *David*, think they can prove the lawfulness of a defensive,

though

though not of an offensive War. For *David*, when he fled from *Saul*, made himself Captain of four hundred men, 1 *Sam*. 22. 2. which number soon increased to six hundred, 1 *Sam*. 23. 13. and still every day increased by new additions, 1 *Chron*. 12. 1. Now why should he entertain these men, but to defend himself against the forces of *Saul*? that is, to make a defensive War whenever he was assaulted by him.

1. In answer to this, I observe, that *David* invited none of these men after him, but they came Volunteers after a Beloved Captain and General; which shews how formidable he could easily have made himself, when such numbers resorted to him of their own accord.

2. When he had them, he never used them for any hostile acts against *Saul*, or any of his forces; he never stood his ground, when he heard *Saul* was coming, but always fled, and his men with him; men who were never used to flie, and were very ready to have served him against *Saul* himself, would he have permitted them. And I suppose they will not call this a defensive War, to flie before an enemy, and to hide themselves in Caves and Mountains;

the Supreme Powers.

tains; and yet this was the onely defensive War which *David* made with all his men about him: nay, all that he would make, and all that he could make, according to his professed Principles, that it *was not lawful to stretch out his hand against the Lord's Anointed*. And when these men are pursued, as *David* was, by an enraged and jealous Prince, we will not charge them with Rebellion, though they flie before him by thousands in a company.

3. Yet there was sufficient reason why *David* should entertain these men, who voluntarily resorted to him, though he never intended to use them against *Saul*: for some of them served for spies to observe *Saul's* motions, that he might not be surprized by him, but have timely notice to make his escape. And the very presence of such a number of men about him, without any hostile Act, preserved him from being seized on by some officious Persons, who otherwise might have delivered him into *Saul's* hands. And he being anointed by *Samuel* to be King after *Saul's* death, this was the first step to his Kingdom, to have such a retinue of valiant men about him; which made his advancement to the Throne more

more easie, and discouraged any oppositions which might otherwise have been made against him; as we see it proved in the event, and have reason to believe that it was thus ordered by God for that very end. It is certain, that *Gad* the Prophet, and *Abiathar* the Priest, who was the onely man who escaped the furie of *Saul* when he destroyed the Priests of the Lord, were in *David*'s retinue; and that *David* enterprized nothing, without first asking counsel of God: But he who had anointed him to be *King*, now draws forces after him, which after *Saul*'s death should facilitate his advancement to the Kingdom.

2. It is objected further, that *David* intended to have staied in *Keilah*, and to have fortified it against *Saul*, had not he been informed that the men of the Citie would have saved themselves by delivering him up to *Saul*, 1 Sam. 23. Now to maintain any strong hold against a *Prince*, is an act of War, though it be but a defensive War. And I grant it is so, but deny that there is any appearance that *David* ever intended any such thing. *David* and his men, by God's appointment and direction, had fought

fought with the *Philiſtins*, and ſmote them with a great ſlaughter, and ſaved *Keilah* from them; and as it is probable, did intend to have ſtaied ſome time in *Keilah*. But *David* had heard that *Saul* intended to come againſt *Keilah*, to deſtroy the Citie, and take him; and enquires of the *Lord* about it, and received an anſwer, that *Saul* would come againſt the Citie. He enquires again, whether the men of *Keilah* would deliver him up to *Saul*, and was anſwered, that they would. And upon this, he and his men leave *Keilah*, and betake themſelves to the ſtrong holds in the Wilderneſs.

But now is it likely, that if *David* had had any deſigne to have fortified *Keilah* againſt *Saul*, he would have been afraid of the men of the Citie? He had 600 men with him in *Keilah*, a victorious Armie, which had lately deſtroyed the *Philiſtins* who oppreſſed them; and therefore could eaſily have kept the men of *Keilah* too in awe, if he had pleaſed, and have put it out of their power to deliver him to *Saul*. But all that *David* deſigned was, to have ſtaid there as long as he could, and, when *Saul* had drawn nigh, to have removed to ſome other place:

place: But when he understood the treacherous inclinations of the men of *Keilah*, and being resolved against all acts of hostilitie, he hastened his remove before *Saul* drew near. So that these men must find some other example than that of *David*, to countenance their rebellion against their *Prince*: for *David* never rebelled, never fought against *Saul*; but when he had a very potent Armie with him, he and his men always fled, and hid themselves in the Wildernefs, and places of difficult accefs.

The fum is this: God from the very beginning, fet up fuch a fupreme and foveraign power in the *Jewifh Nation*, as could not, as ought not to be refifted. This power was at firft in the hands of *Mofes*; and when *Korah* and his companie rebelled againft him, God vindicated his authoritie by a miraculous deftruction of thofe Rebels: *for the earth opened her mouth and fwallowed them up.* Afterward, when they came into *Canaan*, the ordinary exercife of this power was in their *High-Priefts* and *Judges*, whom God raifed up; whofe fentence and judgment was final, and muft not be refifted, under penaltie of death. When the Children of *Ifrael* defired a
King,

the Supreme Powers.

King, this foveraign and irrefiftible power was transferred to him, and fetled in his Perfon. *Saul* was the firft King who was chofen by God, and anointed by *Samuel*; but for his difobedience, was afterwards rejected by God, and *David* the fon of *Jeſſe* was anointed *King* to fucceed after *Saul*'s death: But in the mean time *David* was perfecuted by *Saul*, who fought after his life. And though he himſelf was anointed by God, and *Saul* was rejected by him, yet he durft not refift nor oppofe him, nor defend himſelf by force againft the moſt unjuft violence; but fled for his life, and hid himſelf in Caves and Mountains. Nay, when *Saul* was delivered into his hands by God, he durft not ftretch out his hand againft the Lord's Anointed.

But to proceed in the ſtory. *Solomon*, *David*'s fon, who fucceeded him in his Kingdom, did all thoſe things which God had exprefly forbid the King to do. He fent into *Egypt* for Horſes, 1 *Kings* 10.28. He multiplied Wives, and *loved many ſtrange women, (together with the daughter of Pharoah) women of the Moabites, Ammonites, Edomites, Zidonians, and Hittites*, 1 Kings 11.1. He multiplied

Silver and Gold, 10 *chap* 27. contrary to the command of God. For this God (who is the onely Judge of Soveraign Princes) was very angry with him, and threatens to rend the *Kingdom* from him; which was afterwards accomplished in the days of *Rehoboam:* but yet this did not give authoritie to his Subjects to rebel. If to be under the direction and obligation of Laws, makes a limited Monarchie, it is certain the *Kingdom* of *Israel* was so. There were some things which the *King* was expresly forbid to do, as you have already heard; and the Law of *Moses* was to be the rule of his government, the standing Law of his Kingdom. And therefore he was commanded, when he came to the Throne, *to write a copy of the law with his own hand, and to read in it all his days, that he might learn to fear the Lord his God, and to keep all the words of this law, and these Statutes to do them,* 17 Deut. 18, 19, 20. and yet he was a soveraign Prince: if he broke these Laws, God was his Judge and avenger; but he was accountable to no earthly Tribunal.

Baasha killed *Nadab* the son of *Jeroboam,* and reigned in his stead, 1 *Kings* 15.

the Supreme Powers.

15. 25, 26, 27. and for this and his other sins, God threatens evil against *Baasha*, and against his house, 16 *Chron* 7. *Zimri* slew *Elah* the son of *Baasha*, and slew all the house of *Baasha*; but he did not long enjoy the Kingdom, which he had usurpt by treason and murder: for he reigned but seven days in *Tirzah*; which being besieged and taken by *Omri*, he went into the Palace of the King's house, and burnt the King's house over him with fire, and died, *v.* 18.

This example *Jezebel* threatned *Jehu* with: *Had Zimri peace, who slew his master?* 2 Kings 9. 31. and yet *Nadab* and *Elah* were both of them very wicked Princes. And if that would justifie Treason and Murder, both *Baasha* and *Zimri* had been very innocent.

This is a sufficient evidence, how sacred and inviolable the Persons and Authority of the *Jewish Kings* were, during the time of that Monarchie. But it will not be amiss, briefly to consider what obligations the *Jews* were under to be subject to the higher powers, when they were carried captive into *Babylon*. Now the Prophet *Jeremiah* had given an express command to them, *Seek the peace of the city whither I have*

D 4 *caused*

caused you to be carried away captives, and pray to the Lord for it: for in the peace thereof ye shall have peace, 29 Jer. 7. Which made it a necessary duty to be subject to those powers, under whose government they lived. And accordingly we find, that *Mordecai* discovered the Treason *of Bigthana and Teresh, two of the King's Chamberlains, the Keepers of the door, who sought to lay hand on the King Ahasuerus,* 6 Esther 2. And how numerous and powerful the *Jews* were at this time, and what great disturbance they could have given to the *Empire*, appears evidently from the book of *Esther*. *King Ahasuerus*, upon the suggestions of *Haman*, had granted a Decree for the destruction of the whole People of the *Jews*; which was sent into all the Provinces, written and sealed with the King's ring. This Decree could never be reversed again; for that was contrary to the Laws of the *Medes* and *Persians*. And therefore when *Esther* had found favour with the *King*, all that could be done for the *Jews*, was to grant another Decree for them to defend themselves; which accordingly was done, and the effect of it was this: *That the Jews at Shusan slew three hundred*

dred men, and the Jews of the other Provinces slew seventy and five thousand, and rested from their enemies, 9 Esther 15, 16, 17. Without this Decree, *Mordecai* did not think it lawful to resist, (which yet was a case of as great extremity and barbarous cruelty, as could ever happen) which made him put *Esther* upon so hazardous an attempt, as to venture into the King's presence, without being called; which was death by their Law, unless the King should graciously hold out the golden Scepter to them, 4 *Esth.* 11. and yet when they had obtained this Decree, they were able to defend themselves, and to destroy their enemies; which is as famous an example of *Passive Obedience*, as can be met with in any *History*. And therefore the Prophet *Daniel* acknowledges to *Belteshazzar*, *The most high God gave Nebuchadnezzar thy Father a Kingdom, and Majesty, and Glory, and Honour: and for the Majesty that he gave him, all People, nations, and languages trembled and feared before him. Whom he would he slew, and whom he would he kept alive; and whom he would he set up, and whom he would he pulled down,* 5 Dan. 18, 19. And if these Heathen Kings receive their power from God,

God, as the Prophet here affirms, St. *Paul* has made the application of it, *That he that resisteth, resisteth the ordinance of God.*

This may serve for the times of the Old Testament; and I shall conclude these testimonies with the saying of the wise man, who was both a Prophet and a King: *I counsel thee to keep the King's commandment, and that in regard of the oath of God: Be not hasty to go out of his sight, stand not in an evil thing; for he doth whatsoever pleaseth him. Where the word of a King is, there is power; and who may say unto him, What dost thou?* 8 Eccl. 2, 3, 4.

CHAP.

CHAP. II.

The Doctrine of Christ concerning Non-resistance.

Let us now consider, what Christ and his Apostles taught and practised about Obedience to *Soveraign Princes*; whereby we may learn, how far Christians are obliged by these Laws of *Subjection* and *Non-resistance*.

1. I shall distinctly consider the Doctrine of Christ while he lived on Earth: and here are several things very fit to be observed.

1. We have no reason to suspect, that Christ would alter the rights of Soveraign power, and the measures of obedience and subjection, which were fixt and determined by God himself. This was no part of his Commission, to change the external forms and polities of Civil governments, which is an act of secular power and authority, and does not belong to a *Spiritual Prince*. He who would not undertake to decide a
petty

petty controverſie, or to divide an inheritance between two contending brethren, 12 *Luke* 13, 14. can we think that he would attempt any thing of that vaſt conſequence, as the changes and alterations of Civil Power, which would have unſetled the Fundamental Conſtitutions of all the governments of the world at that time?

Our Saviour tells us, that *he came not to deſtroy the Law and the Prophets, but to fulfil it*, πληρῶσαι, to fill it up, to compleat and perfect it, 5 *Matth.* 17. that is, to fulfil the ancient types and prophecies in his own Perſon, to perfect an external and ceremonial, by a real and Evangelical righteouſneſs, to perfect the Moral Laws with new inſtances and degrees of vertue; but he abrogated no Moral Law, and therefore not the Laws of Obedience and Subjection to *Princes*, which has always been reduced to the fifth Commandment. Nay, he abrogated no Laws, but by perfecting and fulfilling them; and therefore he could make no alteration in the *Doctrine* of *Non-reſiſtance*, which is as perfect ſubjection as can or ought to be paid to Soveraign Princes. His *Kingdom was not of this world*, as he told *Pilate*: though he *the Supreme Powers.* 45

was a King, he neither was an enemy nor rival to *Cæsar*; but had he absolved his Disciples from their obedience to *Princes*, had he made it in any case lawful to resist, (which was so expresly forbid the *Jews* by God himself, and which is such a contradiction to the very notion of Soveraign Power) he had been somewhat worse than a Rival to all the *Princes* of the Earth; for though he had set up no Kingdom of his own, yet he had pulled down theirs. Whereas he took great care, that his Religion should give no disturbance to the world, nor create any reasonable jealousies and suspicions to *Princes*, who had been very excusable for their aversion to Christianity, had it invaded the *Rights* and *Royalties* of their Crowns.

This makes it very improbable that our *Saviour* should make any alterations in Civil powers, or abridge the *rights* of *Soveraignty*; which is so foreign to his design of coming into the world, and so incongruous to the Person which he sustained: and yet he could not alter the duties of Subjects, but he must alter the *rights* of *Princes* too; he must take away the Soveraign power of *Princes*, at the same time that
he

he makes it lawful for Subjects in any case whatsoever to resist. We may safely then conclude, that our Saviour has left the government of the world as he found it: he has indeed given such admirable Laws, as will teach *Princes* to govern, and Subjects to obey better; which is the most effectual way to secure the publick peace and happiness, to prevent the Oppression of Subjects, and Rebellions against *Princes:* but he has not interposed in new modelling the Governments of the world, which is not of such consequence, as some men imagine. It is not the external form of Government, but the Fatherly care and Prudence and Justice of *Governours*, and the dutiful obedience of Subjects, which can make any people happy. If Princes and Subjects be good Christians, they may be happy under most forms of Government; if they be not, they can be happy under none. Had our Saviour given Subjects Liberty to Resist, to Depose, to Murder *Tyrannical Princes*, he had done them no kindness at all; for to give liberty to Subjects to resist, is only to proclaim an universal licence to Factions and Seditions, and Civil Wars; and if any man can think this

such

such a mighty blessing to the world, yet methinks it is not a blessing proper for the *Prince of peace* to give. But he who instructs *Princes* to rule as God's Ministers and Vicegerents, and to express a Fatherly Care and concernment for the happiness of their Subjects, and that teaches Subjects to reverence and obey their *Prince*, as the Image of God, and quietly to submit and yield to his authority, and that inforces these Laws both on Princes and Subjects in the Name and Authority of God, and from the consideration of the future judgment, when Princes who abuse their power shall give an account of it to their great Master, when Subjects who resist shall receive to themselves Damnation, and those, who patiently and quietly suffer for God's sake, shall have their injuries redrest, and their obedience rewarded: I say, such a Person as this, takes a more effectual course to reform the abuses of civil power, and to preserve good government in the world, than all our *wise Politicians* and *State-menders*, who think to reform the government of the world, by some State-spells and charms, without reforming those who govern, and those who are gover-

governed. This our Saviour has done, and this is the best thing that could be done, nay this was all that he could do in this matter. He never usurpt any civil power and authority, and therefore could not new model the governments of the world: he never offers any external force and compulsion to make men obey his Laws, and therefore neither forces Princes to rule well, nor Subjects to obey; but he has taken the same care of the government of the World, as he has done of all the other duties of Piety and Vertue; that is, he has given very good Laws, and threatned those who break them with eternal punishments: and as the Laws and Religion of our Saviour prevail, so will the governments of the world mend, without altering the Model and Constitution of them.

2. But yet we have some positive evidence, what our Saviour taught about Obedience to the higher powers. I shall give you two instances of it, which are as plain and express, as can be desired.

1. The first is, that answer our *Saviour* gave to the *Pharisees* and *Herodians*, when they consulted together to intangle

tangle him in his talk, 22 *Matth.* 15.&c. They come to him with great ceremony and address, as to an infallible Oracle, to consult him in a very weighty case of Conscience. They express a great esteem and assurance of his sincerity, and faithfulness, and courage, as well as of his unerring judgment, in declaring the will of God to them. *Master, we know that thou art true, and teachest the way of God in Truth, neither carest thou for any man, for thou regardest not the Person of man*; that is, thou wilt not conceal nor pervert the truth for fear nor favour: and then they propose an insnaring question to him. *Tell us therefore, what thinkest thou? is it lawful to give Tribute to* Cæsar, *or not?* They thought it impossible that he should give any answer to this, which would not make him abnoxious, either to the *Roman Governours*, if he denied that the *Jews* might lawfully pay Tribute to *Cæsar*, or to the Pharisees and People, if he affirmed that they might: for there was a very potent Faction among them, who thought it unlawful for the *Jews* to own the authority or usurpations of any *Foreign Prince*, or to pay Tribute to him, as to their *King*. They being expresly forbid by their Law, *to set a stranger over them for their King, who is not their Brother,* (*i.e,*) who is not a natural *Jew,* 17 *Deuter.* 15. and it seems they could not distinguish between their own voluntary Act in choosing a stranger for their King, [which was indeed forbid by their Law] and their submitting to a *Foreign Prince,* when they were Conquered by him. Our Saviour, who knew their wicked intention in all this, that they did not come with an honest design to be instructed in their duty, but to seek an advantage against him, expresses some indignation at it: *Why tempt ye me, ye Hypocrites?* but yet to return them an answer to that their question, he bids them shew him the *Tribute-money*, that is, the money in which they used to pay Tribute, and inquires whose Image and Superscription it had. For Coining of money was as certain a mark of Soveraignty, as making Laws, or the power of the Sword. Well, they acknowledge that the Image and Superscription on the Tribute-money was *Cæsars*; upon which he replies, *Render therefore unto Cæsar the things that are Cæsars, and unto God the things that are God's.* The plain meaning of which answer

answer is this, That since by the very impression on their money, it is evident, that *Cæsar* is their *Sovereign Lord*, they must render to him all the *rights* of *Soveraignty*, among which *Tribute* is one, as St. *Paul* tells us, *Render therefore unto all their dues, Tribute to whom Tribute is due, Custom to whom Custom, fear to whom fear, honour to whom honour.* 13 *Rom.* 7. Whatever is due to *Soveraign Princes*, and does not interfere with their duty to God, that they must give to *Cæsar*, who at this time was their *Soveraign*. In which answer there are several things observable.

1. That our Saviour does not examine into *Cæsar's* right, nor how he came by this Soveraign power; but as he found him in possession of it, so he leaves him, and requires them to render to him all the *rights* of *Soveraignty*.

2. That he does not particularly determine, what the things of *Cæsar are*, that is, what his *right* is, as a *Soveraign Prince*. Hence some men conclude, that this Text can prove nothing; that we cannot learn from it, what our Saviour's Judgment was in this point; that it is only a subtil answer, which those who askt the question could make nothing of;

which

which was a proper return to their enſnaring queſtion. This, I think, is as great a reproach to our Saviour, as they can well caſt upon him, that he, who was the wiſdom of God, the great *Prophet* and *Teacher* of Mankind, ſhould return as ſophiſtical and doubtful anſwers, as the *Heathen Oracles*, and that in a caſe, which required, and would admit a very plain anſwer. It is true, many times our Saviour, when he diſcourſt of what concerned his own Perſon, or the Myſteries of his Kingdom, which were not fit at that time to be publiſht in plain terms, uſed a myſtical Language; as when he called his body the *Temple*, or he taught them by *Parables*, which were not obvious at the firſt hearing, but ſtill what he ſaid, had a certain and determined ſenſe, and what was obſcure and difficult, he explained privately to his Apoſtles, that in due time they might explain it to others; but to aſſert, as theſe men muſt do, that Chriſt gave them ſuch an anſwer as ſignifyed nothing, and which he intended they ſhould underſtand nothing by, ſhews that they are not ſo civil to our Saviour as theſe *Phariſees* and *Herodians* were, who at leaſt owned in Complement, *Maſter,*
we

we know that thou art true, and teachest the way of God in Truth, neither carest thou for any man, for thou regardest not the Person of men.

But certainly the *Pharisees* did believe, that there was something in our Saviour's answer; for *they marvelled, and left him, and went their way:* and yet those who had wit enough to ask such ensnaring questions, could not be so dull as to be put off with a sophistical answer, (an art below the gravity of our Saviours Person and Office) but would have urged it a little further, had they not been sensible, that they were sufficiently answered, and had nothing to reply.

For indeed, can any thing be plainer than our Saviour's answer? They ask him, whether it were lawful to pay Tribute to *Cæsar*; he does not indeed in express words say, that they should pay Tribute to *Cæsar*, but he gives them such an answer, as withal convinc'd them of the reason and necessity of it. He asks whose Image and Superscription was on the Tribute-money; they tell him *Cæsar's*; from whence he infers, *Render therefore unto Cæsar the things that are Cæsar's.* Therefore? wherefore? because the Tribute-money had *Cæsar*'s Image on it; therefore they must render to *Cæsar the things that are Cæsar's*; which certainly signifies, that *Tribute* was one of those things which belonged to *Cæsar*, and must be rendred to him, as appeared by it's having *Cæsar*'s Image: not as if every thing that had *Cæsar*'s mark and stamp on it, did belong to *Cæsar*, and must be given to him, (as some men profanely enough, how wittily soever they imagine, burlesque and ridicule our Saviour's answer) for at this rate all the money of the Empire, which bore his Image, was *Cæsar*'s; but the money which was stampt with *Cæsar*'s Image, and was the currant money of the Nation, was a plain sign, as I observed before, that he was their Soveraign, and paying *Tribute* was a known right due to *Soveraign Princes*; and therefore the very money which they used, with *Cæsar*'s Image on it, resolved that question, not only of the lawfulness, but the necessity of paying *Tribute*: and this was so plain an answer, that the *Pharisees* were ashamed of their question, and went away without making any reply; for they no more dared to deny that *Cæsar* was their King, than they thought

thought he dared either to own or deny the lawfulness of paying *Tribute* to *Cæsar*. And this was all the subtilty of our Saviour's answer.

But then our Saviour not confining his answer meerly to the case of paying *Tribute*, but answering in general, that we must render to *Cæsar* the things that are *Cæsar*'s, extends this to all the *rights* of *Soveraign Princes*, and so becomes a standing rule in all cases, to give to *Cæsar* what is *Cæsar*'s due. And when our Saviour commands us to *render to Cæsar the things which are Cæsar's*, without telling us what *Cæsar*'s things are, this is so far from making his answer doubtful and ambiguous, and of no use in this present Controversie, that it suggests to us three plain and natural consequences, which are sufficient to end this whole dispute.

1. That our Saviour did not intend to make any alteration in the rights of *Soveraignty*, but what *rights* he found *Soveraign Princes* possest of, he leaves them in the quiet possession of; for had he intended to make any change in this matter, he would not have given such a general rule, *to render to Cæsar the things which are Cæsar's*, without specifying what these things are. 2. And

2. And therefore he leaves them to the known Laws of the Empire to determine what is *Cæsar*'s right. Whatever is essential to the notion of *Soveraign Power*, whatever the Laws and Customs of Nations determine to be *Cæsar*'s right, that they must render to him; for he would make no alteration in this matter. So that subjection to *Princes*, and *Non-resistance*, is as plainly determined by our Saviour in this Law, as paying *Tribute*; for subjection and *Non-resistance* is as essential a *right* of *Soveraign Power*, and as inseparable from the notion of it, as any thing can be. So it is acknowledged by the Laws and Customs of Nations, and so it is determined by the Apostle St. *Paul*, as I shall shew hereafter.

3. I observe farther, that when our Saviour joyns our duty to our *Prince*, with our duty to our God, *render to Cæsar the things which are Cæsars, and to God the things which are God's*, he excepts nothing from *Cæsar's right*, which by the Laws of Nations is due to Sovereign Princes, but what is a violation of, and an encroachment on Gods right and Soveraignty; that is, we must pay all that Obedience and Subjection to *Princes,*

Princes which is consistent with our duty to God. This is the onely limit our Saviour sets to our duty to *Princes*. If they should command us to renounce our Religion, and worship false Gods; if they should challenge divine honours to themselves, as some of the *Roman Emperours* did; this we must not do, because it is to renounce obedience and subjection to God, who has a more soveraign power, and a greater right in us, than our *Prince*: But all active and passive obedience, which is consistent with a good conscience towards God, and required of us by the Laws of our *Country*, and the essential rights of Soveraignty, is what we owe to our *Prince*, and what by our Saviour's command we must render to him. This I hope is sufficient for the explication of our Saviour's answer to the *Pharisees* and *Herodians*, which evidently contains the Doctrine of obedience and subjection to *Princes*, enforced on us by the authority of our Saviour himself.

2. Our Saviour's rebuke to St. *Peter*, when he drew his sword and struck a servant of the high Priest and smote off his ear, is as plain a declaration against resistance, as words can make it, 26 *Mat.* 52.

rity, if we may oppose unjust and illegal violence, if any obligations of friendship, gratitude, or Religion it self could justifie resistance, St. *Peter* had not met with this rebuke. What should he tamely suffer his Lord and Master to be betrayed, the most admirable example of universal Righteousness and goodness that ever appeared in the world? Shall one who had done no evil, who had neither offended against the Laws of God nor men, who had spent his whole time in doing good, be so barbarously used, and treated like the vilest Malefactor? Shall he who was so famous for miracles, who gave eyes to the blind, and feet to the lame? shall he who was the great Prophet sent from God to instruct the world, shall their dear Master be haled away from them, and they stand by, and see it, & suffer it? Thus might S. *Peter* have argued for himself. But though it was a very unjust action, yet it was done by a just authority: and lawful Powers must not be resisted, though it were in defence of the Saviour of the world. And if St. *Peter* might not use the sword in defence of Christ's Person, there is much less pretence to fight for his religion: for though some call this fighting for religion,

gion, it is onely fighting for themselves. Men may keep their religion, if they please, in despite of earthly powers; and therefore no powers can hurt religion, though they may persecute the Professors of it: And therefore when men take up arms to avoid persecution, it is not in defence of religion, but of themselves, that is, to avoid their suffering for religion. And if St. *Peter* might not fight to preserve Christ himself, certainly neither he nor we might take up arms to defend our selves from persecution. Christ was the first *Martyr* for his own religion; his person was infinitely more sacred and inviolable than any of us can pretend to be. And if St. *Peter* must not fight for Christ, certainly we must not fight for our selves, though we absurdly enough call it fighting for our religion.

And who were these powers St. *Peter* resisted? They were onely the servants and officers of the *High-priest*. The High-Priest did not appear there himself; much less *Pilate*, much less *Cæsar:* and yet our Saviour rebukes St. *Peter* for resisting the inferiour officers, though they offered the most unjust and illegal violence. It seems, he did not understand

stand our modern distinctions between the *Person* and the *Authority* of the *Prince*; That though his person be sacred, and must not be toucht, yet his Ministers, who act by his authority, may be opposed. We may fight his Navies, and demolish his Garrisons, and kill his subjects, who fight for him, though we must not touch his Person. But he is a mock-*Prince*, whose authority is confined to his own Person, who can do nothing more than what he can do with his two hands; which cannot answer the ends of Government. A *Prince* is not meerly a natural, but a Political person, and his personal Authority reaches as far as his commission does. His Officers and Ministers of State, and commanders, and souldiers, are his hands, and eyes, and ears, and legs; and he who resisteth those who act by his commission, may as properly be said to resist the Personal authority of the *Prince*, as if he himself were present in his natural Person, as well as by his authority. Thus our Saviour, it seems, thought, when he rebuked St. *Peter* for striking a servant of the *High-priest*, and smiting off his ear.

And if S. *Peter* were rebuk'd for this, how comes

comes the *Pope* to challenge the sword in S. *Peter*'s right, when our *Saviour* would not allow S. *Peter* to use it himself? And if St. *Peter* might not draw his sword against an inferiour officer, by what authority does the Pope pretend to dispose of Crowns and Scepters, and to trample on the necks of the greatest Monarchs? And I suppose the *Presbyter* can challenge no more authority than the *Pope*. Whether they will allow St. *Peter* to have been a *Bishop* or *Presbyter*, this command to put up his sword, equally concerns him in all capacities, and ought to secure soveraign Princes from the unjust usurpations and treacherous conspiracies both of *GENEVA* and *ROME*.

There is but one Objection, that I know of, against all this from the Doctrine of our Saviour, and that is, that he seems to disallow that very authority which is exercised by *secular Princes*; and therefore cannot be thought such a severe Preacher of obedience & subjection: for Authority and Subjection are correlates, they have a mutual respect to each other; and therefore they must stand or fall together. There is no authority where there is no subjection due, & there can be no subjection due where there is no authority. And yet this is the Doctrine which Christ taught his Disciples, 20 *Mat.* 25, 26, 27, 28 *v. Ye know that the princes of the Gentiles exercise dominion over them, and they that are great, exercise authority upon them. But it shall not be so among you: but whosoever will be great among you, let him be your minister. And whosoever will be chief among you, let him be your servant. Even as the Son of man came not to be ministred unto, but to minister, and to give his life a ransom for many.* This text has been press'd to serve as many ill purposes, as most *texts* in the *Bible*; and therefore deserves to be carefully considered. Some hence infer, that it is unlawful for a Christian to be a *Magistrate*, or a *King*. As if our Saviour either intended that humane societies should be deprived of the advantages of government, which is the greatest temporal blessing and security to mankind; or had made it necessary that some men should continue Heathens and Infidels, that they might govern Christians: which I doubt would be a sore temptation to many to renounce Christianity, if they could gain a temporal Crown by it.

Others from hence conclude, that there

there muſt be no *ſuperiority of degree* between the Miniſters of the Goſpel, but they muſt be all *equal*; as if becauſe the Apoſtles were to be all equal, without any ſuperiority over each other, therefore they were to have no ſuperiority over inferiour Miniſters. As if becauſe the *Apoſtles* might not exerciſe ſuch a ſecular power and ſoveraignty as the *Kings of the Gentiles* did, therefore there muſt be no different degrees of power in the *Miniſters* of the *Church*; that is, that becauſe ſecular and ſpiritual power differ in the whole kind, therefore there are no different degrees of ſpiritual power. As if *Chriſt* himſelf were not ſuperiour to his *Apoſtles*, becauſe he did not aſſume to himſelf the ſecular authority of earthly *Princes*, but came not to be miniſtred unto, but to miniſter, as he commands them to do according to his example.

Others conclude, that at leaſt *Chriſtian Princes* muſt not uſurp ſuch a ſoveraign, and abſolute, and uncontroulable power as the *Princes of the Gentiles* did, but muſt remember that they are but the Publick Servants and Miniſters of the Commonwealth, and may be reſiſted, and called to an account by their
people

people for the male-administration of government. But how they infer this, I confess, I cannot tell: for it is evident our Saviour does not here speak one word in derogation to that civil power and authority which was exercised by *secular Princes.* He tells us indeed, that the *Princes of the Gentiles exercise dominion over them,* and *they that are great, exercise authority upon them:* But does he blame the exercise of this authority? Does he set any narrower bounds or limits, than what the *Heathen Princes* challenged? By no means; he says not one word of any such matter. St. *Matthew* indeed expresses this power of *Princes* by κατακυριεύειν, and κατεξουσιάζειν, which some think intimates the abuse of their Authority: but St. *Luke* renders it by κυριεύειν, and ἐξουσιάζειν, which onely signifies the exercise of *soveraign power.* And though most of the *Roman Emperours* were guilty of very great miscarriages in government, yet our Saviour onely refers to that lawful authority wherewith they were invested, not to the abuse of it: and therefore he takes notice of that honourable Title which was given to many *Roman Emperours*, that they were called Ἐυϵργέται, or Benefactors; which

which certainly does not argue his dislike of civil Authoritie. But all that our Saviour tells his Disciples is, that it should not be so among them, that they should not exercise such a secular power and authoritie as *earthly Princes* do. Now is it any disparagement to *Kingly power*, to tell a *Bishop* that he must not exercise such a soveraign authoritie over the Church, as the *Prince* does over the State ? which is the whole of what our Saviour intended in this place.

For the occasion of these words, St. *Matthew* tells us, was to check that vain ambition of *Zebedee's two sons*, who came to *Christ*, and employed their *Mother* to ask of him, *that one might sit on his right hand, and the other on his left hand, in his Kingdom*; that is, that they might have the greatest places of dignitie and power next himself. St. *Luke* tells us, that it was to compose that strife and contention which was among them, which of them should be accounted the greatest ; which most likely refers to the same story, though it is plain they quarrelled more than once about this matter. And the occasion of all these quarrels, was a mistake of the nature of *Christ's Kingdom*. They, as well as

F 2 the

the rest of the *Jews*, expected their *Messias* should be a *Temporal Prince*; and they being convinced by the Miracles of *Christ*, that he was indeed the *Messias who was to come*, they lived in dayly expectation when he would take the *Kingdom* upon himself; and then they did not doubt but that they should be the *chief Ministers of State*, and have the greatest places of trust and power in his *Kingdom*: & this made them jealous of each others greatness, and so forward to bespeak *preferments* for themselves. Now to cure these earthly ambitions, he tells them, that his *Kingdom* was no such thing as they dreamt of, and that he had no such preferments for them as they expected.

Earthly Princes lived in great Pomp and Splendour, and had great Places of trust and honour to bestow on their servants; but they saw no such thing in him: *he came not to be ministred unto, but to minister*, to live a mean, industrious, and laborious life, and to die as a Malefactor, *and give his life a ransom for many*. And they could not expect by being his servants, to be advanced to secular power and authoritie, which he had not himself; but when he came into his

King-

Kingdom, they should indeed share with him in his power and authoritie: *they should sit upon twelve Thrones, judging the twelve tribes of Israel*; that is, they should have the supreme authoritie in his Church, which is his spiritual Kingdom. But there was nothing of external state and grandeur in this, as they expected; but it was a life of humilitie and modestie, and contempt of this world, and earthly greatness. The greatest Ministers in his Kingdom must be as humble as a child, as he elsewhere tells them, and as diligent and industrious, and condescending, as the meanest servant, and should very often differ nothing from servants in their external fortune and condition of life. This is the sum of what our Saviour here teaches his Disciples; and he is a wonderful man, and very quick-sighted, who can discover any reflection on civil power and authoritie in all this.

I shall onely observe farther, that when our Saviour calls them here, the *Princes* and *Kings of the Gentiles or Nations*, he does not speak this in disparagement of them, that they were onely *Heathen* and *Infidel Princes*, who did this: for there were no other *Princes* at that time in the world. *Heathen* and *Pagan Princes* founds now as a note of infamie, whereby they are diftinguifhed from *Chriftian Kings and Princes*; but the *Kings* of the *Gentiles* or *Nations* in our Saviour's time, fignified no more than *Soveraign Princes*, who were invefted with civil authoritie: And our Saviour onely diftinguifhes between that civil power and authoritie which was exercifed by *fecular Princes*, and that *fpiritual Kingdom* which he was now about to erect in the world; and the diftinction had been of the fame force, though there had been at that time Jewifh or Chriftian, as well as Heathen Princes. Still the difference between Civil and Ecclefiaftical authoritie is the fame; and no Apoftle or Bifhop, as fuch, can challenge the power or authoritie of earthly Princes, or any fhare in it.

CHAP.

CHAP. III.

What we may learn from our Saviour's Practice about NON-RESISTANCE.

Having seen what the Doctrine of our Saviour was, let us now consider his *Practice*. And we need not doubt but our Saviour lived, as he preacht. He taught his Disciples by his example, as well as by his Laws. His Life was the best Comment upon his Sermons, was a visible Lecture of universal Righteousness and goodness; and it is impossible to conceive a more perfect and absolute example of *Subjection* and *Non-resistance*, than our Saviour has set us.

When our Saviour appeared in the world, the *Jews* were very weary of the *Roman yoke*, and in earnest expectation of their *Messias*, who, as they thought, would restore the Kingdom again unto *Israel*; and this expectation of their *Messias*, whom they mistook for a *Temporal*

poral Prince, made them very apt to joyn with any one, who pretended to be the *Messias*, and to rebel against the *Roman* government. Such most likely were *Theudas* and *Judas* of *Galilee*, of whom we have mention, 5 *Acts* 36, 37. and it is not impossible but the *Ægyptian*, who led 4000 men into the wilderness, 2 *Acts* 38. either pretended to be the *Messias*, or some fore-runner of him: to be sure, such were those *false Christs*, and *false Prophets*, of whom our Saviour warns his Disciples, 24 *Matth.* 23. *Then if any man shall say unto you, Lo here is Christ, or there, believe it not*

This being the temper of the *Jewish Nation* at that time, so extreamly inclined to *Seditions*, and *Rebellion* against the *Roman powers*, how easie had it been for our Saviour, had he pleased, to have made himself very potent and formidable! how easie could he have gained even the *Scribes* and *Pharisees* to his party, (whose great quarrel was at his meanness and poverty) would he once have declared himself a *Temporal Prince*, and invaded the Throne! But he was so far from this, that when he perceived the people had an intention to take him by force and make him a King, he withdrew

drew himself privatly from them, *and departed into a mountain himself alone,* 6 *John* 15. and yet I presume, there might have been as many plausible pretences to have justifyed a *Rebellion* then, as ever there were in any *Nation* since. He had at that time fed *five thousand men, besides women and children, with five barley loaves and two small fishes*: and what a formidable Enemy would he have been, who could Victual an Army by Miracles, and could, when he pleased, conquer by the same miraculous power also! this the people, whom he had miraculously fed, were very sensible of, and did hence conclude, that *he was the Prophet that should come into the world,* and that it was time to take him, and set him upon the Throne: but though our Saviour was indeed the *Messias,* yet he was not such a *Messias,* as they expected; he was not a *Temporal Prince,* and therefore would not countenance their *Rebellion* against *Cæsar,* though it were to make himself a *King.*

It is sufficiently known, that Christ submitted to the most unjust sentence, to the most ignominious and painful death, rather than resist the *higher powers,* though he could so easily have *called for*
Le-

Legions of Angels to *his rescue*. But he went as a lamb to the slaughter, and as the sheep before the shearer is dumb, so he opened not his mouth; when he was reviled, he reviled not again; when he suffered he threatned not, but committed himself to him who judgeth righteously. He rebuked *Peter*, when he drew his Sword in his defence, and tells *Pilate* the reason, why he was so easily apprehended, and used at their pleasure, without any resistance and opposition, though he had been formerly attended with such crouds of his *Disciples*; Because he was no *Temporal Prince*, and therefore did not require his *Disciples* to fight for him, as other *Temporal Princes* used to do. *Jesus answered, My Kingdom is not of this world : if my Kingdom were of this world, then would my servants fight, that I should not be delivered to the Jews; but now is my Kingdom not from hence*, 18 *John* 36. Which plainly shews, that our Saviour's subjection was not matter of force and constraint, because he wanted power to resist; but it was matter of choice, that which was most agreeable to the nature of his *Kingdom*, which was not to be propagated by carnal weapons, but by suffering and death.

And

And when our *Saviour* has set us such an example as this, it is wonderful to me, that any, who call themselves his *Disciples*, can think it lawful to *Rebel* against their *Prince*, and defend themselves from the most unjust violence by a more unjust resistance. But there are few men, who are contented to follow Christ to the Cross; they do not like that part of his example, and are willing to perswade themselves, that they are not bound to imitate it. And there are two things, which I find urged by some men to this purpose, which must be briefly considered.

1. That it is no wonder, that Christ suffered patiently and quietly without resisting the most unjust violence, because he came into the world to die, and to make his Soul an offering for sin. And how could so innocent a person die, but by the hands of *unjust* and *Tyrannical powers*? and it was inconsistent with his design of dying for sin, to resist and oppose. This is the account our Saviour himself gives of his patient suffering. When St. *Peter* drew his Sword in his defence, he tells him, *Thinkest thou, that I cannot now pray to my Father, and he shall presently give me more than twelve Le-*

Legions of *Angels* ? But how then shall the Scriptures be fulfilled, that thus it must be ? 26 *Matth.* 43. 54. *And the cup which my Father has given me, shall I not drink it ?* 18 *John* 11. But what is this now to us ? our Saviour did not resist the most *unjust* and *Tyrannical* powers, because God had decreed he should die by their hands, and he came into the world for this very purpose; but has God as peremptorily decreed, that we must suffer also by unjust violence ? were we born for this very end, to suffer death by *Herods* and *Pontius Pilates* ? to be the slaves and Vassals, the scorn and the Triumph of insolent *Tyrants* ? certainly God had a greater care and regard for Mankind than so: and then our case is very different from our Saviour's; and though he died patiently, we may defend our Lives, and our Liberties, which are as dear as our Lives, if we can.

2. And therefore they add, that Christ took upon himself the person not only of a private man, but of a servant, that he might make us free, and that not only as to our Spiritual, but as to our *Civil Liberties,* as the *Virgin Mary* sings; *He hath shewed strength with his arm, he hath scattered the proud in the imagination*

on of their heart: he hath put down the mighty from their seats, and hath exalted them of low degree, 1 *Luke* 51, 52. which they think, does not signifie that Christ has established *Tyrants* in their *Thrones*, and subjected Christians to the vilest slavery. As Christ has taught us by his example to bear servitude and sufferings with an equal mind, when we cannot help it; so he has not forbid us to vindicate and recover our *natural rights* and *liberties*, when we can, according to the express direction of St. *Paul*, *Art thou called being a servant? care not for it: but if thou mayest be made free, use it rather. Ye are bought with a price, be not ye the servants of men*, 1 *Cor.* 7. 21, 23.

Now in answer to this, we may consider in general, that if all this proves any thing, it proves, that *Christ* did not intend, that his sufferings should be an example to us: and yet St. *Peter* expresly tells us, that he did; *Christ also suffered for us, leaving us an example, that we should follow his steps:* & wherein we must imitate Christ in suffering, he tells us in the same place, *viz. in suffering wrongfully, in taking it patiently, when we do well, and suffer for it*, 1 *Pet.* 2. 19, 20, 21.

And

And I think *St. Peter*'s Authority in this case is better then all the Arguments that can be urged against it; and therefore whether we could answer these Arguments or no, yet it is evident, that they are not good, because they prove that which is manifestly false, that Christ is not our Example in suffering, when *St. Peter* tells us, that he is: but yet it is a mighty satisfaction, not only to know, that an Argument is false, but to discover, wherein the fallacy consists; and therefore I shall give a more particular answer to these objections.

1. As for their first Argument, that *Christ* came into the world on purpose to die as a sacrifice for sin, and therefore it was inconsistent with his design, and the person he undertook, to resist and oppose, had it been never so lawful to resist; I grant it is very true, but yet this does not prove, that he cannot be our example in suffering. For,

1. This is not the only reason our Saviour gives of his *Non-resistance*, and patient suffering. He gives *Peter* another reason, Because it is unlawful to draw the Sword against a just Authority, though our cause be never so just: *Put up thy Sword again into his place, for all*

all they that take the sword shall perish by the sword; which I have already explained to you at large. So that our Saviour acknowledges it as unlawful to resist a lawful Authority, as it was inconsistent with his design of dying for the sins of men; and herein certainly he is fit to be our example, in not resisting a lawful Authority in his own defence.

2. I grant, it had not been agreeable to the *Person* which our Saviour took, to have avoided death by a forcible resistance; but then our Saviour voluntarily took such a Person, as was fit to be an example to us. His *Person* and his *Religion* were very well suited to each other; a meek, humble, suffering *person*, to be an example of a meek, humble and suffering *Religion*. His *person* and external circumstances of his appearance were on purpose fitted to his *Religion*; and it is none of the least wonders of the Divine wisdom, that the work of our redemption was accomplisht in such a *mysterious way*, as at once made our Saviour the Author of our redemption, and an example of all the graces and vertues of the Christian life.

Might not these men, if they pleased, by the same Argument prove, that Christ

Christ is not to be our example in meekness and poverty, and contempt of this world, and forgiving enemies, &c. because he came into the world on this design, *not to be miniftred unto, but to minifter?* He chofe a mean and low fortune; and all the affronts and indignities he fuffered, were part of his voluntary *humiliation*, and therefore it became him to bear them patiently, and to forgive them, as much as it did to die patiently by wicked hands; but there is not the fame reafon for us to do fo: and thus it will be hard to find any thing, wherein Chrift is to be our example, becaufe the very reafon of his coming into the world, the manner and circumftances of his appearance, all that he did and fuffered, may be refolved into the decree and appointment of God, and his voluntary undertaking, and the accomplifhment of ancient *Types* and *Prophecies*; and therefore he is no more to be an example to us, than a man who acts the part of a *beggar* or of a *Prince*, is to be an example to all that fee him.

But methinks it is worth confidering, why *Chrift* chofe fuch a perfon as this. Why he was born of mean and obfcure parents, and chofe a poor and induftrious life,

life, and an accursed and infamous death? was it impossible for *infinite wisdom* to have laid a more glorious and triumphant scene of our redemption? was there no possible way, but the condescension and sufferings of his own Son? Let those say that, who dare venture to determine, what infinite wisdom can do. It is enough for me to know, that Christ took such a mean and suffering person upon him, because it was most agreeable to the Religion, which he preacht, and of which he was to be an example; and therefore though Christ suffered for other reasons, and to other ends and purposes, than we do or can suffer, yet his sufferings are an example to us, because God chose to save and redeem us by the sufferings of his Son, not only that he might expiate our sins by his blood, but also that he might be an example to us of mecknefs, and patience, and submission to the Divine will, and subjection to government, even in the most unjust and infamous sufferings.

3. We may consider further, that *Christ's* suffering in obedience to the will and appointment of God, does not make him unfit to be our example. For

though God has not so peremptorily decreed, that all Christians should suffer, as he did that Christ should suffer, yet whenever we are called forth to suffer, (as we always are, when we cannot avoid suffering without resisting a lawful Authority) our sufferings are as much the effects of God's decree and appointment, as the sufferings of Christ were; and in such cases every *Christian* may, and ought to say, as his Lord did, *The Cup which my Father hath given me shall I not drink it?* Thus St. *Peter* expresly tells the *Christians* to whom he wrote, and gives it as a reason, why they should suffer patiently, *even for doing well. For even hereunto were you called, because Christ also suffered for us, leaving us an example, that we should follow his steps*, 1 *Pet.*2.21. Now *calling* in the *New Testament* signifies the *choice* and *election* of *God*, and always supposes a divine *decree*, *appointment*, and *constitution*, as the foundation of it. Thus St. *Paul* tells us, that the gifts and calling (κλῆσις) of God are without repentance, 11 *Rom.* 29. that is, that decree he made to choose the posterity of *Abraham* for his people, which still intitled all those of them to the blessings of the Gospel, who would believe

lieve in *Chrift*. Thus the state of Chriftianity is our calling, and holy calling, 2 *Tim*. 1. 9. 3 *Heb*. 1. becaufe it is the *way* and *means* God hath chofen and appointed for the Salvation of Mankind: and Chriftians are often ftiled the *Called*, becaufe God has now decreed to chufe all the fincere Difciples of Chrift, as he formerly did the pofterity of *Abraham*, to be his peculiar people; and throughout the Scriptures of the New Teftament, God is never faid to *call*, nor any one to be *called of God*, but with refpect to fome divine *decree* and *conftitution*; and therefore when St. *Peter* tells the Chriftians, that they are *called to fuffer*, it fignifies that God has appointed them to it, by his pofitive will and decree.

This St. *Paul* difcourfes more at large in his Epiftle to the *Romans*, and comforts them under their fufferings from this very confideration, that the fufferings which they underwent, were not the effects of meer chance and accident, nor of the wickednefs and injuftice of men, nor barely of Gods permiffion, but of his decree and appointment; and therefore they might certainly conclude, that what ever their fufferings were, they fhould turn to their good,

8 *Rom.* 28, 29, 30. *And we know that all things work together for good to them that love God, to them that are called according to his purpose,* τοῖς κατὰ πρόθεσιν κλητοῖς, *to those who are called,* that is, to suffer, which is the argument the *Apostle* is discoursing of, according to his will and pleasure and appointment.

Sufferings are not for the good of all profest Christians, for they may tempt Hypocrites to renounce their Religion, and great and severe sufferings may be too powerful a temptation for weak though sincere Christians; and therefore when the rage and malice of men boils and swells, God sets bounds to it, and does not suffer these persecutions and afflictions promiscuously to light upon all Christians, but exerciseth a very particular providence in chusing out fit persons to suffer, in directing the storm and tempest of Persecution to fall where he pleases, upon such Persons, who are armed with faith and patience to resist its fury, and to bear and conquer its rage. And such persons, who are thus appointed, who are thus *called* by God to suffer, shall be sure to conquer, and to receive the reward of Conquerours. For thus the Apostle adds, *For whom he did*

did foreknow, he also did predestinate to be conformed to the Image of his Son, that he might be the first-born among many brethren. This conformity to the Image of Christ in this place, does plainly signifie a conformity to him in sufferings, as is evident from the whole scope of the place. Some persons it seems there are, whom God does predestinate or fore-appoint to be conformed to the sufferings of Christ: for this is not the actual portion of all Christians, though it is the condition of our Discipleship; and they are those whom he did foreknow. Now the fore-knowledge of God includes his choice and election; he chuses out of the body of Christians, some fit persons to make his Martyrs and Confessors, to be examples of Faith and Patience and Courage to the world, *And whom he did predestinate, them he also called; and whom he called, them he also justified; and whom he justified them he also glorified*; that is, those persons whom God thus chuses, and preordains to suffer as Christ did, in time he calls forth to suffer; and when he does so, he *justifies* them, that is, he brings them off with triumph and victory, and owns and applauds their Faith and Patience. For so δικαιω sometimes signifies; and therefore to be *justified*, is expounded by to conquer and overcome, 3 *Rom.* 4. *That thou mightest be justified* (ινα δικαιωθῇς) *in thy sayings, and mightest overcome when thou art judged.* And indeed this is properly to be *justified* in any trial or combate, to overcome and conquer; and that God who gives the victory, gives the reward too: and whom he *justifies*, them he also *glorifies:* which seems to refer not to those rewards which are common to all Christians, but to some peculiar degree of glory, which is prepared for such Conquerours, as the Apostle speaks; *If so be, that we suffer with him, that we may be also glorified together,* 17 v.

So that though God has not made us slaves and vassals to the humour of every Tyrant, yet all the afflictions and sufferings of Christians, especially those, which befal them on the account of Religion, are as particularly ordered and determined by God, as the sufferings of Christ himself were: and therefore there is no difference upon this account between the sufferings of Christ, and the sufferings of his Disciples; and therefore though Christ came into the world on purpose to suffer in obedience to the Di-

Divine will, this does not make him ever the less fit to be an example to us. Nay, his obedience to the will of God in suffering the hardest things from the most unjust and Tyrannical powers, is an example to us of the same patient suffering, and submission to the will of God.

It is true, none of us in particular can know that God has decreed, that we shall suffer such or such things, and from such or such hands, as our Saviour did; but yet this we know, that it is God's will and pleasure, that we should patiently endure those sufferings, which we cannot avoid without sin; and since he has forbid us by express Laws to resist the higher powers, whatever sufferings cannot be avoided without resistance, it is God's will and pleasure, that we should submit to them. And since none of these sufferings, which are unavoidable to us, befal us without the particular decree and appointment of God, we have reason in imitation of our great Master, to submit to them with the same cheerfulness and self-resignation as he did.

There is something indeed in the example of our Saviour, which in our cir-

circumstances we are not bound to imitate. For he punctually knowing, what God's will and pleasure was concerning him, voluntarily chose that condition, which he so well knew, God had allotted for him. He freely chose a mean and servile fortune, he chose suffering and death; when his time of offering up himself was come, he went up to *Jerusalem* on purpose to die there: but we are not bound to choose poverty and disgrace and suffering, we are not bound. voluntarily to deliver up our selves into the hands of *Tyrants* and *Persecutours*, who thirst after our Blood. We may and ought to use all just and honest arts to make our condition easie and comfortable in the world, and to avoid the rage and fury of bloody men, because we cannot tell, that it is the will and appointment of God, that we shall suffer, till our sufferings are unavoidable: and then when we must either suffer or sin, when we must either renounce our Religion, or resist the powers, we must embrace suffering and death, as that portion, which God has allotted for us.

I shall onely observe, by the way, what a mighty security this is to all good Christians, how *absolute* or *tyrannical*

nical soever the power be under which they live; that they are safe in God's hands, and all the Powers of men and Devils cannot touch them, till God by a positive decree appoints and orders their suffering. There could not be greater nor more absolute *Tyrants* than the *Roman Emperours* were at this time, and yet they had no power over the meanest Christian, but by an express commission from Heaven. This is the special priviledge of the Christian Church above the rest of mankind, that they are God's peculiar care and charge; that he does not permit any sufferings or persecutions to befal them, but what he himself orders and appoints. It is a great security to the World, that there is no evil happens to men but what God permits, and that he permits nothing but what he can over-rule to wise and good ends; but it is a greater happiness to have our condition immediately allotted by God. God may permit a great many evils to befal us in anger and displeasure; but when he takes us into his immediate protection, and under his own government, whatever evils he appoints for us, whoever are the instruments of them, are certainly

tainly for our good: and therefore there is no such danger in the Doctrine of *Non-resistance,* as some men imagine. How *absolute*soever this may be thought to render *Princes,* sincere Christians can suffer nothing by it: for they shall suffer nothing, more nor less, than what God appoints for them to suffer.

2. It is also urged against the obligation of our Saviour's example to suffer as he did, that Christ by his state of servitude and sufferings, has purchas'd liberty for us; and that not onely a spiritual and internal, but an external and civil liberty. We are no longer bound to submit to *usurping* and *tyrannical* powers, when we have strength and power to deliver our selves from that necessity. There is no help for it, but men who are weak and unable to resist, must obey and suffer; but this is matter of force, not of duty: We are now bought with a price, and therefore must not chuse a state of subjection and servitude to men.

1. Now in answer to this, we may consider first, that this obedience and subjection to *Soveraign Princes,* either was a duty before Christ's appearing in the world, or it was not. If it were not,

not, then our deliverance from this subjection to *Princes*, is no part of that liberty which Christ has purchas'd for us, because it was the natural right of mankind before; and therefore there was no need of Christ's dying to purchase this, which he cannot give us a greater right to than we had before his death. If subjection and *Non-resistance* were our duty before, and ceases to be our duty now, then Christ by his death has cancelled the obligations of our duty, and purchas'd a liberty and freedom not to do that now which by the Laws of God or Nature we were bound to do before; that is, Christ by his death has abrogated not onely the Ceremonial, but some Moral Laws; which I shew'd you before was contrary to the nature and designe of his undertaking.

2. It is strangely unaccountable, how obedience to any Law should abrogate and cancel it. How Christ by subjection to the higher powers, should for ever after deliver his Disciples from the necessity of subjection, and make them free from the authority and government of *Princes*, whenever they dislike their government. A typical Law may be fulfilled and receive its just accomplishment,

plishment, and then its obligation ceases. Thus the death of Christ fulfilled the Levitical sacrifices, and put an end to them: But the authority of a moral Law is confirmed and strengthened, not abrogated and disanulled by great examples. When Christ quietly and patiently submitted to the most unjust sentence, in obedience to lawful authoritie, he either did well or ill in it: If he did ill, his example indeed is not to be imitated; but if he did well, how did his doing well deliver us from the obligation of doing well? Did his doing well, make it ill for us to do as he did? Why did not his perfect and unsinning obedience as well deliver us from the obligation of all the other Laws of God, as from obedience and subjection to *Princes*?

The *Antinomians* indeed are so absurd as to say, that Christ fulfilled all righteousness in our stead, and that every believer has fulfilled the Law in Christ; and therefore is not bound to fulfil it in his own person as a condition of life and salvation. But yet they are not so absurd as to say that Christ by the righteousness of his life and death, has altered the nature of good and evil, and cancelled

celled any one Law of God. The Law is in force still, and the dutie is the same; but the Law cannot take hold of them, nor exact a personal righteousness from them, because they have already fulfilled the Law in Christ. But now these men must say, that Christ has not onely fulfilled the Law of *subjection* and *non-resistance*, as a condition of salvation, but has cancelled it as a rule of life.

3. The death of Christ could not purchase any civil rights or liberties which we had not before, nor make any change in the external fortunes or conditions of men. The death of Christ is represented in Scripture either as an atonement or expiation of sin, or as the purchase and seal of the new Covenant. Now how does the death of Christ, by expiating our sins, deliver us from subjection to our civil Governours? What connexion is there between the expiation of our sins, and our freedom from the authoritie of Princes, that he who does one, must be supposed to do the other?

And as for the new Covenant, where does that grant any new franchises and liberties to subjects? Let them produce their new Charter to justifie their exemption

emption from subjection to *Princes*; let them shew any one saying in the Gospel of our Saviour, if they can, to that purpose. What the Doctrine of Christ is, you have already heard; and when Christ died to confirm the new Covenant in his bloud, it is absurd to say that he has purchased any liberties for us, but what he has expresly granted to us in his Gospel.

He does indeed promise libertie & freedom to his subjects, but it is a libertie of another nature; a libertie from the power and dominion of sin. *Ye shall know the truth, and the truth shall make you free,* 8 John 32. that is, the power of the Gospel-revelation should deliver them from the Empire of their lusts, and give them the true government and masterie of themselves: And therefore he adds, *Verily, verily, I say unto you, Whosoever committeth sin, is the servant of sin. And the servant abideth not in the house for ever: but the son abideth for ever. If the son therefore shall make you free, ye shall be free indeed,* 34, 35, 36 v.

But does not St. *Paul* advise the Corinthians to assert even their civil and political freedom when they can, and that from this argument, that they are

the

the freemen of Christ? which seems to intimate, that there is such a connexion between our spiritual and civil Liberties, that it does not become Christ's freemen to be slaves and servants unto men. 1 Cor. 7. 21, 22, 23 v. *Art thou called, being a servant? care not for it: but if thou mayest be made free, use it rather. For he that is called in the Lord, being a servant, is the Lord's free man: likewise also he that is called, being free, is Christ's servant. Ye are bought with a price, be not the servants of men.*

But what is it they would prove from these words? that our subjection to men is inconsistent with our freedom in Christ? that the Apostle expresly denies. *For he that is a servont, is Christ's freeman.* Or that Christ, when he made us free, did deliver us from the subjection of men? not that neither. For he does not advise Christian servants to leave their masters, as he might and ought to have done, if Christ had bestowed this civil libertie on them; but he was so far from this, that when *Onesimus* had run away from his Master *Philemon*, and was converted by St. *Paul*, and proved very useful and serviceable in the ministrie, yet he would not detain

tain him from his Master, without asking his leave: which occasioned the Epistle to *Philemon*, as you may see 10, 11, 12, &c. And in this place he advises the Christian servants not to be concerned at their being servants; which was no injury at all to their Christian libertie: But if they could procure their libertie by any fair and just means, they should chuse to do it; which is upon many accounts more desirable, especially when Christians were servants to heathen Masters, as it often was in those days.

But does not the Apostle expresly tell them, Ye are bought with a price, be not ye the servants of men? Yes, he does: but sure this cannot signifie that servants should cast off the authoritie of their Masters. For that is directly contrary to what he had advised them before, and contrary to his own practice in the case of *Onesimus*, whom he sent back to his Master *Philemon*. But all that I understand by it, is this; that those Christian servants who could not obtain their freedom, should yet take care not to be servants to the lusts and passions of their Heathen Masters. For though a state of civil bondage and slavery

slavery is not inconsistent with their Christian libertie, yet to be ministers and servants to the vices of men, is: And therefore when they lay under any such temptation (as Christians who served Heathen Masters could not long escape it) they must then remember that they are Christ's freemen, who were bought with a price; and therefore must neither be servants to their own lusts, nor to the lusts of other men. And the reason why I chuse this sence of the words, is this; because the *Apostle* opposes being bought with a price, that is, their being redeemed by Christ, or being Christ's freemen, to their being the servants of men, as inconsistent with each other. And therefore their being the servants of men, cannot be understood of civil servitude, which he before had told them was not inconsistent with their Christian libertie, but of being servants to the vices of men.

But what now is all this to subjection to *Soveraign Princes?* Does the Apostle exhort the Christians too to throw off the civil powers? It was possible for a Christian servant to purchase his libertie, or to obtain it some other lawful ways; but how can subjects deliver themselves from the authoritie of Princes? unless they go into some Country where there is no government, or resist and rebel against the higher powers where they are: Neither of which is agreeable to our Apostles Doctrine, who would not allow servants to run away from their Masters, much less rebel against them to procure their libertie.

Nor was the case the same between Christian subjects and soveraign Princes, and between Masters and Servants; and therefore neither is the reason the same, why subjects should desire freedom from the higher powers. Servants in those days were slaves and vassals, and were kept in such constant attendance on their Masters, that it must needs be very difficult; besides the other temptations they were exposed to, to gain any time or libertie for attending on Christian Worship, and the instructions of the Church. But Christian subjects are more at their own disposal, even under *Heathen Princes*; and have all that libertie, excepting the case of persecution, which is necessary for the purposes of Religion; which yet is the onely reason intimated here, why the Apostle advises servants to procure their freedom, if they can. To

To conclude this Argument; there were a sort of men, even in the Apostles days, who boasted mightily of their Christian libertie, and thought scorn for a Christian either to be a servant or a subject. For this reason St. *Paul* in this place instructs servants, that their Christian libertie is not injured by their being servants: for this reason are there such frequent directions to servants to obey their Masters. For this reason does St. *Peter* caution the Christians against this pretence of Christian libertie, which some abused then, as they do still, to the disturbance of civil governments; *As free, but not using your liberty for a cloak of maliciousness, but as the servants of God.*

CHAP. IV.

What St. Paul Preached about Non-resistance of the Higher Powers.

Having thus concluded what the Doctrine and Example of our Saviour was, about subjection to the higher powers; let us now consider the Doctrine and Example of his Apostles. Not as if the Authority and Example of our Saviour were not sufficient of it self to make a Law, but stood in need of the confirmation and additional authority of his own Apostles; but we might justly suspect our selves mistaken in the meaning of our Saviour's words, or in the intention and design of his sufferings, had none of his Apostles, who were immediately instructed by himself, and acquainted with the most secret mysteries of his Kingdom, ever preacht any such Doctrine as this, of *Subjection* to *Princes*. And therefore to give you the more abundant assurance of this, I shall plainly shew you, that the Apostles taught the same Doctrine, and imitated the example of their great Master.

I shall begin with St *Paul*, who has as fully declared himself in this matter, as it is possible any man can do by words, 13 Rom. 1, 2. *Let every Soul be subject unto the higher Powers: for there is no power but of God: the Powers that be, are ordained of God Whosoever therefore resisteth the power, resisteth the ordinance of God; and they that resist, shall receive to themselves damnation.*

This is a very express Testimony against Resistance, and therefore I shall consider it at large; for there have been various Arts used to pervert every word of it, and to make this Text speak quite contrary to the design and intention of the Apostle in it: and therefore I shall divide the words into three general parts.

1. The Doctrine, the Apostle instructs them in: *Let every Soul be subject to the higher powers.* 2. The reason whereby he proves and inforces this Doctrine: *For there is no power but of God; the powers that be, are ordained of God. Whosoever therefore resisteth the power, resisteth the ordinance of God* 3. The punishment of such resistance: *And they that resist, shall receive to themselves damnation.*

1. I shall begin with the Doctrine, *That every Soul must be subject to the higher powers.* And here are three things to to be explained. 1. Who are contained under this general expression of *every Soul.* 2. Who are meant by *the higher powers.* 3. What is meant by being *subject.*

1. Who are contained under this general expression of *every Soul,* πᾶσα ψυχὴ. which by an ordinary Hebraism, signifies every man. For man is a compounded Creature of Body and Soul, and either part of him is very often in Scripture put for the whole. Sometimes Flesh, and sometimes Soul signifies the man; and when *every Soul* is opposed to the *higher powers,* it must signifie all men, of what rank or condition soever they be, who are not invested with this higher power. *Popes* and *Bishops* and *Priests,* as well *Spiritual* as *Secular persons;* the whole body of the People, as well as every single individual. For when *every Soul* is commanded to be subject, without any exception or limitation, this must reach them in all capacities and conditions.

The design of the Apostle, as you shall hear more presently, was to forbid all re-

resistance of *Soveraign P*...
he known of any...
men, who might law...
not to have exprest it in such general
terms, as to forbid all without exception. Had St. *Paul* known the Prerogative of St. *Peter*, and his Successors the *Bishops* of *Rome*, would he have written to the Christians of *Rome* to be subject to their *Emperours*, without making any provision for the greater Authority of their *Bishops*?

The reason he assigns why every Soul must be subject to the *higher Powers*, is, *because all powers are of God*. So that whoever is bound to be subject to God, must be subject to their *Prince*, who is in God's stead. And this I think will reach the *Pope of Rome*, as well as any private Christian; unless he will pretend to more authority on earth, than God himself has: for the *Prince* has God's Authority, and therefore cannot be resisted, but by a greater Authority than God's. And by the same reason, if the whole body of the people be subject to God, they must be subject to their *Prince* too, because he acts by God's Authority and Commission. Were a Soveraign *Prince* the Peoples Creature,
that

might be a good Maxime, *Rex major singulis, sed minor universis*, that the King is greater than any particular Subject, but less than All together; but if he be God's Minister, he is upon that account as much greater than all, as God is.

And that the whole body of the people, all together, as well as one by one, are equally concerned in this command of being subject to the *higher Powers*, is evident from this consideration, that nothing less than this will secure the peace and tranquillity of humane Societies. The resistance of single persons is more dangerous to themselves than to the Prince, but a powerful combination of Rebels is formidable to the most puissant Monarchs. The greater numbers of Subjects rebel against their Prince, the more do they distress his Government, and threaten his Crown and Dignity: and if his Person and Authority be Sacred, the greater the violence is, which is offered to him, the greater is the crime.

Had the Apostle exhorted the *Romans* after this manner: Let no private and single man be so foolish, as to rebel against his *Prince*, who will be too strong for him: but if you can raise sufficient forces

forces to oppose against him, if you can all consent to Depose or Murder him, this is very innocent and justifiable, nay an Heroical Atchievement, which becomes a free-born people: How would this secure the peace and quiet of the world? how would this have agreed with what follows, that *Princes* are advanced by God, and that to resist our *Prince*, is to resist the Ordinance of God, and that such men shall be severely punisht for it in this world or the next? for can the Apostle be thought absolutely to condemn resistance, if he makes it only unlawful to resist when we want power to conquer? Which yet is all that can be made of it, if by every Soul the Apostle means only particular men, not the united force and power of Subjects.

Nor can there be any reason assigned, why the Apostle should lay so strict a command on particular Christians to be subject to the higher Powers, which does not equally concern whole Nations. For if it can ever be lawful for a *whole Nation* to resist a *Prince*, it may in the same circumstances be equally lawful for a particular man to do it: if a Nation may conspire against a *Prince*, who invades

vades their Rights, their Liberties, or their Religion, why may not any man by the same reason resist a *Prince*, when his Rights and Liberties are invaded? It is not so safe and prudent indeed for a private man to resist, as for great and powerful numbers; but this makes resistance only a matter of discretion, not of Conscience: if it be lawful for the whole body of a Nation to resist in such cases, it must be equally lawful for a particular man to do it; but he does it at his own peril, when he has only his one single force to oppose against his *Prince*. So that our Apostle must forbid resistance in all or none. For single persons do not use to resist or rebel, or there is no great danger to the *Publick* if they do; but the Authority of *Princes*, and the security of publick Government, is only endangered by a combination of *Rebels*, when the whole Nation or any considerable part for numbers, power, and interest, take Arms against their Prince. If resistance of our Prince be a sin, it is not the less, but the greater sin, the greater and the more formidable the resistance is; and it would very much unbecome the gravity and sacredness of an Apostolical precept,

cept, to enjoyn subjection to private Christians, who dare not, who cannot resist alone; but to leave a powerful combination of Rebels at liberty to resist. So that *every Soul* must signifie *all Subjects* whether single or united: for whatever is unlawful for every single Person considered as a Subject, is unlawful for them all together; for the whole Nation is as much a subject to the *higher powers*, as any single man. Thus I am sure it is in our Government, where *Lords* and *Commons* assembled in *Parliament* own themselves the Subjects of the *King*, and have by publick Laws disclaimed all power of raising any *War* either *offensive* or *defensive against the King*.

2. Let us now consider what is meant by the higher powers, [ἐξουσίαις ὑπερεχούσαις] which signifies the supreme power in any Nation, in whomsoever it is placed. Whether in the *King*, as in *Monarchical governments*; or in the *Nobles*, as in *Aristocratical*; or in the *People*, as in *Democracies*. At the time of writing this Epistle, the supreme power was in the *Roman Emperours*; and therefore when St. *Paul* commands the Roman Christians to be subject to the *higher powers*, the plain meaning is, that they
should

be subject to the *Roman Emperour*. And thus St. *Peter* explains it, 1 *Epist.* 2 *Chap.* 13 *v.* Be subject to every ordinance of man for the Lord's sake, whether to the *King* as supreme, ὡς ὑπερέχοντι, the word used in my *Text*, as to him who hath a supereminent power, and is above all others.

It is absolutely necessary in all well-governed Societies, that there should be some supreme and soveraign Power, from whence there lies no appeal, and which cannot and must not be resisted. For otherwise there can be no end of disputes, and controversies; men may quarrel eternally about rights and priviledges, and properties, and preheminencies; and when every man is Judge in his own cause, it is great oddes but he will give Judgement for himself, and then there can be no way to determine such matters, but by force and power. Which turns humane societies into a state of War, and no man is secure any longer, than he happens to be on the prevailing side.

Whoever considers the nature and the end of Government, must acknowledge the necessity of a supreme power, to decide controversies, to administer Justice, and

and to secure the Publick Peace: and it is a ridiculous thing to talk of a supreme power, which is not *unaccountable and irresistible. For whatever* power is liable to be called to an account, and to be resisted, has some power above it, and so is not supreme.

Of late years, whoever has been so hardy, as to assert the Doctrine of *Nonresistance*, has been thought an Enemy to his Country, one who tramples on all Laws, who betraies the rights and liberties of the subject, and sets up for Tyranny and Arbitrary power. Now I would desire those men, who think thus, to try their skill in framing any model of government, which shall answer the ends and necessities of humane society, without a supreme power, that is, without such a power, as is absolute and unaccountable.

If there be no supreme power in any society, when ever there happens any difference among the members of such a society, nothing can be done; and such a society is an arbitrary and voluntary, not a governed society; because there is no body to govern, and no body to be governed: they may govern themselves by mutual consent; but if they cannot agree,

agree, there is an end of their government.

Where there is any government, there must be some-body to govern, and whoever has the power of government, must not be contradicted or resisted, for then he cannot govern; for a power to govern men onely when, and in what cases they please to be governed, is no power. Now place this power where you will, in a single Person, or in the hands of some select persons, or in the people, and the case is the same; where ever the power rests, there it is absolute and unaccountable: wherever there is any government, there must be a last appeal, and where the last appeal is, whether to a *Prince*, to a *Parliament*, or to the *People*, there is soveraign and absolute power, which cannot be resisted without a dissolution of government, and returning to a state of war; which is a direct contradiction to the first institution of humane societies, and therefore that which cannot be allowed by the fundamental constitutions of any society.

The result of all in short is this: 1. That in all civil governments, there must be some supreme and soveraign power. 2. That the very notion of supreme

supreme power is, that it is unaccountable and irresistible. And therefore, 3. whatever power in any nation according to the fundamental laws of its government, cannot and ought not to be resisted, that is the supreme power of that nation, the higher powers to which the Apostle requires us to be subject. And from hence it is evident, that the *Crown of England is an Imperial Crown*, and has all the rights of Soveraignty belonging to it. Since according to the fundamental Laws of the Realm, 'the *Person* and *Authority* of the *King* is sacred and irresistible. The *Oaths* of *Allegiance* and *Supremacy*, those Laws which declare and acknowledge the *King* to be supreme in his Dominions under God, to have the sole power of the Sword, that it is Treason to levy War against the *King* within the *Realm*, and without; That both or either *Houses* of *Parliament* cannot, nor lawfully may, *raise* or *levy war offensive* or *defensive* against his *Majesty*, his *Heirs*, or *lawful Successors* ; That it is not lawful upon any pretence whatsoever to take Arms against the *King*, and that we must abhor that traiterous position of taking arms by his authority against his *Person*, or against those who

who are commissionated by him: These, I say, and such like declarations as these, both formerly and of late, made by both *Houses of Parliament*, and enacted into publick laws, are a sufficient proof, that the supreme power of these Realms is lodged in the *Prince*. For he who is unaccountable and irresistible is supreme.

But to avoid all this, there are some who tell us, that by the higher powers in the Text, the Apostle means the Law. For laws are the highest and most venerable authority in any Nation; and we ought indeed to be subject to *Princes* who themselves are subject to the Laws, which they are as much obliged to by virtue of this Apostolical command as meaner Persons. For the law is as much superior to them, as they are to their own subjects; and therefore when *Princes* violate publick laws, they are no longer to own them for the *Higher Powers*, but may vindicate the laws against them, may defend the legal authority of their *Prince* against his Personal usurpations, may fight for the Authority of the *King* against his *Person*.

But in answer to this, we may consider, 1. That it is evident from the whole context and manner of speaking, that

that the Apostle does not here speak of laws, but Persons; not of Imperial laws, but soveraign Princes. Laws were never before called the *higher Powers*, neither in sacred nor profane writers; ἐξουσία in the new Testament always signifies the authority of a Person, not of a law. And hence it signifies the Person invested with this authority. It were easy to prove this by numerous instances; but it will be sufficient to shew, that thus it must signifie in the Text. These are such powers as are of God, appointed and ordained by God; which I suppose does not signifie the laws of every nation, many of which are far enough from being divine. They are expresly called Rulers in the 3 v. and are the object of fear; which can punish and reward: *if thou wilt not be afraid of the power,* ἐξουσία, *do that which is good, and thou shalt have praise of the same.* Now I think no law, but the *Power*, which executes laws, can apply punishments or rewards according to mens deserts: and in the 4 v. this very power is called the *Minister of God*, and said to bear the sword, which does not belong to laws but Persons; and in the Text the Apostle speaks of resisting these

these powers, opposing force to force. Now though laws may be disobeyed, it is onely lawgivers and Rulers, who are capable of resistance.

2. But however, these higher Powers may signifie Princes and Rulers, as governing according to known laws. No, this cannot be neither, because the Apostle speaks of such powers as were under the government of no laws; as it is sufficiently known the *Roman Emperours* were not; their will was their law, and they made or repealed laws at their pleasure. This Epistle was wrote either under *Claudius* or *Nero*; and I think I need not tell you, that neither of those *Emperours* had any great Reverence for laws, and yet these were the higher powers to whom the Apostle commands them to be subject: and indeed, though there be a vast difference between a *Prince*, who by the fundamental Constitutions of his Kingdom, ought to govern by laws, and a *Prince* whose will is his law; yet no law can come into the notion and definition of supreme and soveraign Powers: such a Prince is under the direction, but cannot properly be said to be under the government of the law, because there

is

is no superior power to take cognizance of his breach of it; and a law has no authoritie to govern, where there is no power to punish. But I shall have occasion to discourse this more largely hereafter.

3. Let us now consider, what is meant by being subject. Now subjection, according to its full latitude of signification, includes all those duties, which we owe to soveraign Princes; a chearful and willing obedience to all their Just and lawful commands; an humble submission to their reproofs and Censures, Corrections and punishments; to honour and Reverence their Persons and Authority; to pay custom and tribute, and all legal taxes and impositions, as our Apostle addes, verse the 7. *Render therefore unto all their dues, tribute to whom tribute is due, custom to whom custom, fear to whom fear, honour to whom honour.* But the principal thing he has regard to in the text, is *Non-resistance*, which is the onely perfect and absolute subjection we owe to Princes. We are not always bound to do what they command, because they may command, what we ought not, what we must not do; but we are always bound

to be subject, that is, never to resist. Though a *Prince* abuse his power, and oppress his subjects, we must not take upon us to right ourselves, but must leave our cause to God, who is the great Protector of opprest Innocence: for as the Apostle tells us, He *that resisteth the power, resisteth the ordinance of God; and they that resist,* &c. This is the doctrine the Apostle teaches, that *we must be subject to,* that is, that we must not resist, nor rebel against *soveraign Princes.*

2. Let us then now consider the reason, whereby the Apostle proves and inforces this doctrine of *subjection* or *Non-resistance.* *For there is no power but of God: the powers that be, are ordained of God. Whosoever therefore resisteth the power, resisteth the ordinance of God.* The plain meaning of which is this: That *soveraign Princes* are advanced to the Throne by God, and are his ministers and vicegerents, invested with his authority and power to govern; and therefore when we resist our *Prince,* we resist the ordinance, constitution, and appointment of God. Such men do not resist, rebel, or fight against man, but God. As he who resists any subordinate

ordinate Magistrates, resists his Prince, from whom they receive their authority and commission. And this is a very forcible Argument to *subjection* to *Princes:* for whatever our *Prince* be, it is certain, that God has an absolute and uncontroulable right over us, as being the natural Lord and Governour of the world; and if Earthly *Princes* are plac't in the Throne by him, who is at liberty to put the Government of the world into what hands he pleases, who will dare to oppose God? or ask him, Why hast thou done so? Whoever has any sense of God's dominion and soveraignty, dares not rebel against him; and he, who believes that *Princes* are made by God, will no more dare to rebel against his *Prince*, than against God himself.

The *Patrons* of *resistance* have used all manner of arts to evade the force of this *Text*, and to make the *Apostles* argument signifie just nothing; and therefore it will be necessary to consider briefly what they say.

1. Then some of them own the truth of what St. *Paul* asserts, that *Soveraign Princes* are of God, are advanc't and set in their Thrones by him; but then they say, *Princes* are from God, no other-

Milton pro Pop. Angl. defensio. p. 68.

wise than every thing else is of God. The divine Providence governs all things; and Plague and Pestilence and Famine, and whatever evil and calamity befals a nation, is from God too; but does it hence follow, that when God brings any of these Judgements upon us, we must not Endeavour to remove them? No more, say they, does it follow, that we must not Endeavour to break the Yoak of a *Tyrant*, because it was put on by God. That is, in plain English, that when the *Apostle* proves, that we must not resist *Princes*, because they are set up by God, he does not reason truly; for notwithstanding this, we may resist *Tyrannical Princes*, as we would do the *Plague*, though they are both sent by God: and I suppose these men believe that St. *Paul* was no more inspired by God, than *Princes* are made by him. Otherwise they might as easily have concluded, that since St. *Paul* founds no doctrine of *Non-resistance* upon God's authority and dominion in advancing *Princes*, (and his argument must be good, if he were an inspired man) that therefore there is some little difference between God's making a *King* though a *Tyrant*, and
his

his sending the plague: and any man of an ordinary understanding might guess, that when God sets up a *King* with a soveraign Power, he sets him up to govern; and therefore though he may prove a scourge and a Plague, yet he is such a Plague, as God will allow no man to remove, but himself. For it is a contradiction in the nature of the thing, to give authority to a *Prince* to govern, and to leave subjects at Liberty to resist. *Tyrants* are God's mininisters, though they be but Executioners of his just vengeance; but an Executioner, though he be as dangerous as the Plague, cannot be resisted, without resisting the *Prince*.

2. At other times they tell us, that when St. *Paul* asserts, that *there is no power but of God, the powers that be, are ordained of God,* he means this onely of the Institution of civil power and government, not of every *Prince* that is advanced to this power. The institution of civil government they will allow to be from God, but they think it a reproach to God to own that *Tyrants* and oppressors, wicked and impious Kings, are advanced by God. His Providence many times, for wise reasons,

permits

permits this, as he does all other evils; but they cannot believe, that such men are advanc't by his council and approbation, and positive will and appointment. But this admits of various answers. For,

1. Can there be no wise reason given, why God may advance a bad man to be a *Prince*? If there may, then it is no reproach to the divine Providence. The natural end of humane societies is the preservation of Publick Peace and order; and this is in some measure attained even under the government of *Tyrants*. But God has a further end than this, to bless and reward a virtuous Nation, or to punish a loose and degenerate age; and there cannot be a greater blessing than a wise and virtuous *Prince*, nor a greater plague than a Merciless *Tyrant*: and therefore the Providence of God is as much concerned in setting a good or a bad *Prince* over any people, as in rewarding or punishing them. Upon this account, God calls the *King* of *Assyria the rod of his anger, whom he raised up for the punishment of an Hypocritical Nation,* 10 Isai. 5, 6.

2. I have already proved, that by the

the *Powers* in my *Text*, the *Apostle* means the persons of *Soveraign Princes*; and therefore according to his Doctrine, those *Princes* who were then in being, that is, the *Roman Emperors*, were advanc't by God; *the powers that be*, that is, the *Princes* and *Emperors* who now govern the world, are ordained and appointed by God. And that thus it is, God himself tells us, 27 Jerem. 5, 6. *I have made the Earth, and given it unto whom it seemed meet unto me: and now I have given all these lands into the hands of Nebuchadnezzar King of Babylon my servant.* Thus he called *Cyrus* by name, many years before he was born, *to be his shepherd, and to perform his pleasure in rebuilding Jerusalem*, 44 Isa. 28. 45. ch. 1, 2, 3, 4.

This was the belief of the primitive Christians under heathen and persecuting *Emperors*. *Tertullian* who wrote his *Apologie* under *Severus*, asserts that *Cæsar* was chosen by God, and therefore that the Christians had a peculiar *Propriety* in *Cæsar*, as being made *Emperor* by their God. *Sed quid ego amplius de religione atque pietate christiana in Imperatorem, quem necesse est suspiciamus, ut eum quem Dominus noster elegit, & merito*

rito dixerim, noster est magis Cæsar, a Deo nostro constitutus. Tert. Apol. cap. 33. and this he assigns as the reason, why they honour and reverence, and pray for him, and are in all things subject to him,

3. If these men will grant, the institution of civil power and authority by God is a necessary reason why we must not resist those who have this power, it shall satisfie me; and I will dispute no further, whether by *Powers* in the *Text* the *Apostle* means civil government, or the Persons of *Princes*, so long as the Doctrine of *Non-resistance* is secured: but if they will not grant this, then they must grant, that either the *Apostle* reasons weakly, or that this is not the sense of his words.

St. *Chrysostom* indeed by the *Powers* that be ordained of God, understands no more than that civil power and authority is from God, as being afraid to own that all *Princes*, though never so wicked are appointed by God; but then he owns the doctrine of *Non-resistance*, because the power is from God, whoever have the possession of it, or however he came by it. But I think the argument for *Non-resistance* is much stronger,

ſtronger, if we acknowledge, that *ſoveveraign Princes* themſelves are appointed by God, and have this power put into their hands by his peculiar and ordering Providence.

4. Others in plain terms deny, that this is true, that Princes receive their power from God, and are ordained and appointed by him, though the words of the Apoſtle are very plain and expreſs in the caſe.

But let us ſet aſide the Authority of the *Apoſtle* a while, and examine why they ſay ſo. And this they think is very plain in all Nations, that *Princes* are advanc't to the Throne by the choice and conſent of the *People*, or by *right* of *inheritance*, confirmed and ſettled by *publick Laws*, which include the conſent of the *People*, and therefore they receive their power from thoſe who choſe them; which is no more than a *Fiduciary power*, which they are lyable to give an account of to thoſe who chooſe them.

Now grant this to be true, that *Princes* are advanc't to the Throne by the *People*, which will not very well hold in *conqueſts*, nor in *hereditary Kingdoms*; yet, I ſay, ſuppoſe it to be true,
ſince

since it was manifestly the case of the *Roman Empire*, when the Apostle wrote this Epistle, their *Emperors* being chosen either by the *Senate* or the *Army*; yet I would desire to be resolved in some few plain questions.

1. Whether God does nothing, but what he does by an immediate power? Whether he cannot appoint and choose an *Emperor*, unless he does it by a *Voice* from Heaven, or sends an *Angel* to set the Crown upon his head? Whether God cannot by a great many unknown ways, determine the choice of the *people*, to that *Person*, whom he has before chosen himself? May we not as well say, that God does nothing but miracles, because every thing else has some visible cause, and may be ascribed either to natural or moral agents? God may chuse an *Emperor*, and the *people* chuse him too, and the *peoples* choice is onely the effect of *God's* choice; and therefore notwithstanding all this, *Princes* owe their crowns and scepters to *God: the powers that be are ordained of God.*

2. How does it follow, that because *Princes* are chose by the people, therefore they derive their power from them, and are accountable to them? This is
not

not true in humane governments. A City or any Corporation may have Authority to choose their Magistrates, and yet they do not derive their power from their fellow-Citizens, who chose them, but from their *Prince*. Thus the *People* may chuse, but God invests with power and Authority. For indeed, how can people, who have no power of Government themselves, give that power, which they have not? God is the only governour of the world, and therefore there can be no power of Government, but what is derived from him. But these men think, that all civil authority is founded in consent; as if there were no natural Lord of the world, or all mankind came free and independent into the world. This is a contradiction to what at other times they will grant, that the institution of Civil power and Authority is from God; and indeed if it be not, I know not how any Prince can justifie the taking away the life of any man, whatever crime he has been guilty of. For no man has power of his own life, and therefore cannot give this power to another: which proves that the power of capital punishments cannot result from meer consent, but from a

fusuperiour Authority, which is Lord of life and death.

If it be said, that every man has a natural right to defend his own life by taking away the life of any man who injuriously assaults him, and he may part with this power of self-defence to his *Prince*, and that includes the power of life and death: I answer,

1. Suppose the Laws of *Self-preservation* will justifie the taking away another man's life in preservation of our own, yet this is a *Personal right*, which *God* and *Nature* has given us; and unless we can prove, that we have Authority to make over this *right* to another, as well as to use it our selves, our consent cannot give Authority to the Magistrate to take away any man's life in our cause.

2. This natural right of self-defence cannot be the Original of the Magistrates power, because no man does give up this right. Every man has the right of *Self-preservation*, as intire under civil government, as he had in a state of Nature. Under what government soever I live, I may still kill another man, when I have no other way to preserve my own life from unjust violence by private hands

hands. And this is all the liberty any man had in a supposed state of nature. So that the Magistrates power of the Sword is a very different thing from every man's right of self-preservation, and cannot owe its original to it. For,

3. The Magistrates power of the Sword is not meerly *defensive*, as the right of self-preservation is, but *vindicative*, to execute vengeance on evil doers; which power no man has over his equals in a state of Nature. For vengeance is an act of superiority, and supposes the Authority of a Lord and Judge; and therefore the consent of all Mankind cannot give the power and authority of a Sword to a *Prince*, because they never had it themselves. A *Prince*, as he bears the Sword, is not the peoples Officer, but the Minister of God, a revenger to execute wrath upon him that doth evil, as our Apostle adds, *v.* 4. and this is the true reason of our subjection. *Wherefore you must needs be subject, not only for wrath, but also for conscience sake.*

4. There is another objection against what the Apostle affirms, that *there is no power but of God: the powers that be, are ordained of God.* For is the power of victorious Rebels and Usurpers from God?

God? did *Oliver Cromwell* receive his power from God? then it seems, it was unlawful to resist him too, or to conspire against him: then all those Loyal Subjects, who refused to submit to him, when he had got the power in his hands, were Rebels and Traitors.

To this I answer, that the most prosperous Rebel is not the *Higher Powers*, while our *natural Prince*, to whom we owe obedience and subjection, is in being. And therefore though such men may get the power into their hands by Gods permission, yet not by Gods Ordinance; and he who resists them, does not resist the Ordinance of God, but the usurpations of men. In *Hereditary Kingdoms*, the *King* never dies, but the same minute that the natural Person of one *King* dies, the Crown descends upon the next of Blood; and therefore he who rebelleth against the Father, and murders him, continues a Rebel in the Reign of the Son, which commences with his Fathers death.

It is otherwise indeed, where none can pretend a greater right to the Crown, than the *usurper*; for there possession of power seems to give a right. Thus many of the *Roman Emperours* came to the

the Crown by very ill means, but when they were possest of it, they were the *Higher Powers*: for the Crown did not descend by *inheritance*, but sometimes by the *Election* of the *Senate*, sometimes of the *Army*, and sometimes by *force* and *power*, which always draws a consent after it. And therefore the *Apostle* does not direct the Christians to enquire by what Title the Emperours held their Crowns, but commands them to submit to those, who had the power in their hands: for the possession of Supream and Soveraign power is *Title* enough, when there is no better *Title* to oppose against it. For then we must presume, that God gives him the irresistible authority of a *King*, to whom he gives an irresistible power; which is the only means, whereby *Monarchies* and *Empires* are transferred from one Nation to another. There are two Examples in Scripture which manifestly confirm what I have now said.

The first in the Kingdom of *Israel*: after the ten Tribes had divided from the House of *Judah*, and the Family of *David*, God had not entailed the Kingdom upon any certain Family; he had indeed by *Abijah* the Prophet promised after *Solomons* death ten Tribes to *Jeroboam* the Son of *Nebat*, 1 *Kings* 11. 29. &c. but had afterwards by the same Prophet threatned *Jeroboam*, to destroy his whole Family, *Chap.* 15. 10, 11. *Baasha* fulfils this prophecy by the traiterous murder of *Nadab*, (who succeeded his Father *Jeroboam* in the Kingdom) and usurpt the government himself, and slew all *Jeroboam's house*, 28, 29. *v*. This Murder and Treason is numbred among the sins of *Baasha*; for which God afterwards threatned to destroy his house, as he had done the house of *Jeroboam*, 16 *Chap. v.* 7. and yet he having usurpt the Throne, and got the power into his hands, and no man having a better Title than his, God himself is said to have exalted him out of the dust, and made him *Prince* over his *People Israel*, *v*. 2. *Elah* succeeded *Baasha*, who had no better Title than his Father; and yet *Zimri*, who slew him, is accused of Treason for it, *v* 20. *Zimri* usurpt the Kingdom when he had slew his Master, but he was only a vain pretender to it, when he wanted power; for when the people who were encamped against *Gibbethon*, heard that *Zimri* had killed the King, they made *Omri* King, and went immediately

the Supreme Powers. 131

diately and besieged *Tirzah*, where *Zimri* had taken possession of the Kings Palace; who finding no way to escape, set fire to it himself, and died in the flames of it. And now *Israel* was divided between *Omri* and *Tibni*; but those who followed *Omri* prevailed against those who followed *Tibni*; and *Tibni* died, and *Omni* Reigned, *v.* 21, 22. All which plainly shews, that where there is no regular Succession to the Kingdom, there possession of power makes a King, who cannot afterwards be resisted and opposed without the guilt of treason: and this was the case of the *Roman Empire*, at the writing of this Epistle; and therefore the Apostle might well say, *That the powers that be, are ordained of God.* That whoever had the Supream power in his hands, is the higher power, that must not be resisted.

But it was otherwise in the Kingdom of *Judah*, which God himself had entailed on *Davids* Family, as appears from the example of *Joash*, who was concealed by his *Aunt Jehosheba*, and hid in the house of the Lord for six years. During this time *Athaliah* reigned, and had the whole power of government in her hands; but yet this did not make

K 2 her

her a Soveraign and irresistible *Prince*; because *Joash* the Son of *Ahaziah*, the right Heir of the Crown, was yet alive. And therefore in the seventh year *Jehoiada* the Priest set *Joash* upon the Throne, and slew *Athaliah*, and was guilty of no Treason or Rebellion in doing so, 2 *Kings* 11. Which shews, that no usurpations can extinguish the Right and Title of a natural *Prince*. Such Usurpers, though they have the possession of the supream power, yet they have no right to it; and though God for wise reasons may sometimes permit such usurpations, yet while his Providence secures the Persons of such deposed and banished Princes from violence, he secures their Title too. As it was in *Nebuchadnezzar*'s vision; *The tree is cut down, but the stump of the roots is left in the earth. The Kingdom shall be sure to them, after that they shall know, that the Heavens do rule*, Dan. 4. 26.

3. The Apostle adds the punishment of those, who resist the *higher Powers*: *They that resist, shall receive to themselves damnation.* Where, by judgment and damnation, it is plain the Apostle means the punishments of the other world. Prosperous Rebellions are not always punisht in this world, but they are in the next.

next. And therefore we must be subject not only for wrath, for fear of men; but out of Conscience towards God, and a reverence of his righteous judgments.

The sum of all in short is this. That all men, whatever their rank and condition be; not only Secular, but Spiritual Persons; not only private men, but subordinate Magistrates; not only single men, but whole Bodies and Communities, the united force and power of a Nation, must be subject to *Soveraign Princes*; that is, must obey all their just and lawful commands, and patiently submit even to their unjust violence, without making any resistance, without opposing force to force, or taking Arms, though it be only in their own defence. For *Soveraign Princes* are made and advanced by God, who exerciseth a particular providence in the disposal of Crowns and Scepters, and over-ruleth all external and second causes, to set up such *Princes* as he himself has first chose; and therefore he that resisteth, resisteth not Man, but God; he opposeth the constitution and appointment of the Soverain Lord of the world, who alone is our natural Lord and Governour, and who alone has right to put the government of the world into what hands he pleases; and how prosperous soever such Rebels may be in this World, they shall not escape the Divine Vengeance and Justice, which will follow them into another world: *they shall receive to themselves Damnation.*

This was St. *Paul*'s Doctrine about subjection to the *higher powers*; and he did not only preach this Doctrine himself, but he charges *Timothy* and *Titus*, two Bishops whom he had ordained, the one *Bishop* of *Ephesus*, the other of *Crete*, to preach the same.

Thus he charges *Titus*, *to put them in mind to be subject to Principalities and Powers, to obey Magistrates, to be ready to every good work,* 3 *Titus* 1. When he commands him to put them in mind to be subject, he supposes, that this is a known duty of the Christian Religion, and a duty of such great weight and moment, that people ought to be frequently minded of it; that the Bishops and Ministers of Religion ought frequently to preach of it, and to press and inculcate it upon their hearers. For it is a great scandal to the Christian Religion, when this duty is not observed: and yet in in many cafes this duty is fo hard to be obferved, & requires fuch a great degree of felf-denial and refignation to the will of God, and contempt of prefent things, that too many men are apt to forget it, and to excufe themfelves from it. And therefore St. *Paul* gives this in particular charge to *Titus*, and in him to all the Bifhops and Minifters of the Gofpel, to take fpecial care to inftruct people well in this point, and frequently to renew and repeat their exhortations; efpecially, when they find a bufie, factious, and feditious fpirit abroad in the world.

Thus he inftructs *Timothy* the *Bifhop* of *Ephefus*, 1 *Tim*. 2. 1. *I exhort therefore, that firft of all, fupplications prayers, interceffions, and giving of thanks, be made for all men; for Kings, and for all that are in authority, that we may lead a quiet and peaceable life, in all godlinefs and honefty.*

But you will fay, What is this to fuch an abfolute fubjection to Princes as includes *Non-refiftance* in it? cannot we pray for any man, without making him our abfolute and Soverain Lord? are we not bound to pray for all our Enemies and Perfecutors? and does our praying for them, make it unlawful to refift and oppofe oppose their unjust violence? How then can you prove from the duty of praying for Kings, that it is in no case lawful to resist them? if it were lawful to resist *Tyrannical Princes*, yet it might be our duty to pray for them. And therefore though it be our duty to pray for *Princes*, it does not hence follow, that we may in no cases lawfully resist them.

In answer to this, I grant, that praying for any man, nay praying for *Kings* and *Princes* cannot of it self prove, that it is unlawful to resist them, if it otherwise appear, that resistance is lawful; but if it be our duty to make supplications, prayers, and intercessions for persecuting *Princes*, as the Apostle commands them to pray for the *Roman Emperors*, who were profest enemies to Christianity; that is, if they must beg all good things for them, a long and happy and prosperous Reign, which is included in intercessions and prayers; this strongly infers, that they must not resist their power, nor undermine their Thrones. For we cannot very well at the same time pray for the prosperity of their government, and endeavour to pull it down. The Apostle did not understand those conditional Prayers, that God would *Convert*

vert or *Confound* them; a *prayer*, which thanks be to God, was never found in any Christian *Liturgie* yet; which possibly is one reason, why some men are no great Friends to *Liturgies*. And when the Apostle directs them to *pray for Kings and all that are in authority, that they must live quiet and peaceable lives in all godliness and honesty*, that is, that they might enjoy peace and security in the profession and practice of the true Religion; this seems to imply, that when they are persecuted for their Religion, which was the case at that time, they must pray for persecuting Princes, that God would incline their hearts to favour his people; but must not fight against them. This is the only direction the Apostle gives them in the case; and we may reasonably suppose, that had he known any other, he would not have concealed it. If it is always the duty of Christians to pray for the prosperous and flourishing state of the *Empire*, as by this Apostolical exhortation it appears to be, it could never be lawful for them to resist the powers: for I cannot understand how any man without mocking Almighty God, can pray for the prosperity of his Prince, and the good

suc-

success of his government, at the same time, when he fights against him. When St. *Paul* had so freely and openly declared against resisting the higher powers, which *Timothy*, who was his Scholar and Companion, and fellow-labourer, could not but know; what other interpretation could he make of the Apostles exhortation, to pray for Kings, and all that are in authority, that we may live quiet and peaceable lives in all godliness and honesty, but only this, that prayer is the last and only remedy that we can have against persecuting *Princes?* Had it been lawful for them to resist, it had been a more proper prayer, that God would give them strength and courage and counsel to oppose all his and their enemies: that he would appear as miraculously for their defence, as he formerly did in fighting the *Battels* of *Israel*; that he would set Christ upon his Throne, and make all the *Princes* of the earth give place to a more glorious Kingdom. Time was, when it was all one, whether he saved with many or a few. He knew how to destroy potent and formidable Armies, without any humane strength and power, or by such weak & contemptible means, as reserved the

the glory of the victory intire to himself: and he is the same still that ever he was, and his power is the same. But St. *Paul* very well knew, that it was not lawful for them to pull Emperours out of their Thrones, to give any disturbance to civil powers, or to attempt any changes or innovations in government; and therefore since they must submit to such Princes as they had, there was no other remedy left them, but to beg of God so to incline the hearts of Princes, that they might enjoy a quiet and peaceable possession of their Religion, even under Pagan Princes. For as much as some men of late days profanely scoff at prayers and tears, these have been always thought the onely remedy the Church has against persecuting powers; and it seems St. *Paul* thought so too, for he prescribes no other; and yet he does not allow them to pray against the King neither, but exhorts them to pray for him, and that they might enjoy peace and security under his Government.

CHAP.

CHAP. V.

St. Peter's Doctrine about Non-resistance.

Having heard what St. *Paul's* doctrine was, let us now consider what St. *Peter* taught about this matter: he had as much reason to learn this lesson as any of the Apostles; our Saviour having severely rebuked him for drawing his sword against the lawful powers, as you have already heard. And indeed, his rash and intemperate zeal in this action cost him very dear; for we have reason to believe, that this was the chief thing, that tempted him to deny his *Master*. He was afraid to own himself to be his Disciple, or that he had been in the garden with him; because he was conscious to himself, that by drawing his sword, and smiting the servant of the high Priest, he had incurred the penalty of the law, and had he been discovered, could expect nothing less, but to be severely punish't for it, it may be to have lost his life for his

his refiftance. And indeed, this has very often been the fate of thofe men, who have been tranfported with a boiftrous and intemperate zeal to draw their fwords for their Mafter and his Religion againft the lawful powers, that they commonly deny their Mafter, and defpife his Religion, before they put their fwords up again.

But St. *Peter* having by our Saviour's reproof, and his own dear-bought experience learn't the evil of refiftance, never drew his fvvord more, and took great care to inftruct Chriftians not to do fo, 1 Peter 2. 13, 14, 15, 16. *Submit your felves to every ordinance of man for the Lord's fake, whether it be to the King as fupreme; or unto Governours, as to them that are fent by him, for the punifhment of evil doers, and for the praife of them that do well. For fo is the will of God, that with well doing, ye may put to filence the ignorance of foolifh men. As free, and not ufing your liberty as a cloak of malicioufnefs, but as the fervants of God.*

This is the very fame Doctrine, which St. *Paul* taught the Romans: *Let every foul be fubject to the higher Powers*; for the fame word is ufed in the ori-

original ὑποταγή and ὑποτάσσεσθαι, and therefore to submit and to be subject is the same thing, which, as St. *Paul* tells us, signifies *Non-resistance*. Onely as St. *Paul* speaks onely of not resisting the *Higher Powers*, that is, *Emperours* and *Soveraign Princes*, herein including all those, who act by their Authority; St. *Peter*, to prevent all cavils and exceptions, distinctly mentions both, that we must submit to all humane power and authority, not onely to the *King as Supreme*, that is, in St. *Paul's* phrase, to the *Higher Powers*, to all *Soveraign Princes* who are invested with the supreme Authority; but also to those, who *are sent by him*, who receive their Authority and commission from the *Soveraign Prince*.

St. *Paul* tells us at large, that *all power is of God*, and that the power is the *Minister of God*, and *he that resisteth the power, resisteth the ordinance of God*; and *therefore we must needs be subject, not onely for Wrath*, that is, for fear of being punish't by men, *but also for Conscience sake*, out of reverence to God, and fear of his Judgement. This St. *Peter* comprises in one word, which includes it all; Submit your selves to every ordinance of man *for the Lord's sake*: for how

how is God concerned in our obedience to *Princes*, if they be not his Ministers, who are appointed and advanced by him, and act by his Authority, and if it be not his will and command, that we should obey them? and therefore he addes, for *this is the will of God, that with well doing*, that is, by obedience and subjection to Princes, *ye may put to silence the ignorance of foolish men*, that is, that you may put to silence those foolish men, who ignorantly accuse you, as fond of changes, and troublesome and dangerous to Government. But then St. *Peter* observing, that Christian Liberty was made a pretence for seditions and treasons, he cautions them against that also, *As free, but not using your liberty for a cloak of Maliciousness*, that is, to cover and excuse such wickedness as Rebellion against Princes, *but as the servants of God*: You must remember, whatever freedom Christ has purchas't for you, he has not delivered you from obedience and subjection to God; you are his servants still, and therefore must be subject to those, who receive their power and authority from God, as all *Soveraign Princes* do.

This is as plain, one would think, as words

words can make it; but nothing can be so plain, but that men who are unwilling to underſtand it, and who ſet their wits on work to avoid the force and evidence of it, may be able to find ſomething to ſay, to deceive themſelves, and thoſe who are willing to be deceived: and therefore it will be neceſſary to conſider, what falſe colours ſome men have put upon theſe words, to elude and baffle the plain ſcope and deſigne of the Apoſtle in them.

As firſt, they obſerve, that St. *Peter* calls *Kings* and ſubordinate Governours an ordinance of man, or a humane Creature, ἀνθρωπίνη κτίσις. and from hence they conclude that *Kings* are onely the *peoples Creatures*; they are made by the *people*, and receive their power from them, and therefore are accountable to them if they abuſe their power. In anſwer to this, we may conſider,

1. That this interpretation of St. *Peter's* words, is a direct contradiction to St. *Paul*, who expreſly aſſerts, that there is no power but of God, the powers that be are ordained of God: but according to this expoſition of *humane Creature*, or the *Ordinance of Man*, there is no power of God, but all power is derived from the

the Supreme Powers.

the *People*. Kings and Princes may be chosen by men, as it is in *Elective Kingdoms*, and as it was at that time in the *Roman Empire*; but they receive their power from God, and thus St. *Paul* and St. *Peter* may be reconciled: but to affirm, that St. *Peter* calls Kings an Ordinance of man, because they receive their power and authority from men, is an irreconcilable contradiction to St. *Paul*, who affirms, that they receive their power from God, that they are God's and not the peoples Ministers. Now though St. *Peter* and St. *Paul* did once differ upon a matter of prudence, it would be of ill consequence to Religion, to make them differ in so material a Doctrine as this is: and yet there is no way to reconcile them, but by expounding St. *Peter's* words so as to agree with St. *Paul's*; for St. *Paul's* words can never be reconciled with that sence, which these men give of St. *Peter's*; and that is a good argument to me, that is not the true interpretation of St. *Peter*; for I verily believe, that these two great Apostles did not differ in this point.

2. St. *Peter* exhorts them to *submit to every ordinance of man for the Lord's sake,*

L

sake; which plainly signifies, that whatever hand men may have in modelling civil governments, yet it is the Ordinance of God, and *Princes* receive their power from him. For it is no act of disobedience to God to resist our *Prince*, nor of obedience to God to submit to him, if he does not derive his power from God, and act by his Authority and commission; especially in such cases, when he opposes the Government of God, and the interest of Religion; and oppresses not onely God's Creatures, but his most faithful and obedient people, who are his peculiar care and charge: in such cases as these, if *Princes* do not receive their power from God, they are opposite and rival Powers, and we can no more submit to them for God's sake, than we can submit to a Rebel for the sake of, that is, out of duty and loyalty to our *natural Prince*. And therefore when the Apostle exhorts them, for God's sake to submit to their King, he plainly supposes, what St. *Paul* did particularly express, that Kings receive their power from God, and therefore are God's Ministers, even when they abuse their power; and he that resists, resists the Ordinance and Authority of God.

3. But

3. But suppose we should grant, that when St. *Peter* calls Kings the Ordinance of man, he means, that they receive their power and authority from men; yet I cannot see, what good this will do them: for he plainly disowns their consequence, that therefore *Princes* are accountable to the People, as to their superiours, and may be resisted, deposed, and brought to condigne punishment, if they abuse this power; as will appear from these two observations. 1. That he gives the King the Title of *supreme*, ὑπερέχοντι, who is above them all, and is invested with the supreme and soveraign power. Now the supreme power in the very notion of it, is irresistible and unaccountable; for otherwise it is not supreme, but subject to some superiour jurisdiction; which it is evidently known the *Roman Emperours*, of whom the Apostle here speaks, were not. And 2. that he requires subjection to this humane ordinance, which, as appears from St. *Paul*, signifies *Non resistance*. So that though we should grant that the *King* derives his power from the people, yet it seems, God confirms and establishes the Crown on his head, and will not suffer people to take it off again, when they please.   L 2   4. But

4. But after all, there is no colour for this objection from the Apostles words: for this ἀνθρωπίνῃ κτίσει humane order or ordination, signifies nothing but humane authority, such power and authority as is exercised by men for the good government of humane Societies. And the meaning is only this; that out of reverence and obedience to God, from whom all power is derived, they should submit to that authority, which is exercised by men, whether to the supream power of *Soveraign Princes*, or that subordinate authority which he bestows on *inferiour Magistrates*.

2. It is farther objected, that though St. *Peter* does command Christians to submit to Kings and Governours, yet it is with a limitation, as far as they govern well, while they exercise their authority in pursuance of the great ends of its institution; *for the punishment of evil doers, and for the praise of them that do well.* And here St. *Peter* agrees very well with St. *Paul*, who assigns this as the reason, why they may be subject to the powers: For *Rulers are not a terrour to good works, but to the evil; wilt thou then not be afraid of the power? do that which is good, and thou shalt have praise*

praife of the fame. For he is the minifter of God to thee for good. But if thou do that which is evil, be afraid, for he beareth not the fword in vain: for he is the minifter of God, an avenger to execute wrath upon him that doth evil, 13 Rom 3, 4. Now we cannot be bound to obey and fubmit, any farther than the reafon of our obedience reaches: and if the reafon why we muft obey Princes, is, becaufe they punifh wickednefs, and reward and encourage Vertue, which is fo great a bleffing to humane Societies, then we are not bound to obey them, when they do quite contrary; when they encourage Vice, and opprefs the moft exemplary innocence. Now in anfwer to this, let us confider,

1. Whether thefe great Apoftles intended to oblige the Chriftians of that age to yield obedience to thofe powers, which then governed the world. If they did, (as I think no man will be fo hardy as to fay, that they did not) then it will be proper to enquire, whether what they here affirm, and affign as the reafon of their fubjection, that *Rulers are not a terrour to good works, but to the evil*, were true of the *Roman Emperours* and Governours, or not. If it

were true, then I believe it will hold true of all *Kings*, in all ages of the world; for there cannot well be greater *Tyrants* than the *Roman Emperors* were at this time: and so this will prove an eternal reason, why we should be subject to *Princes*, notwithstanding the many faults and miscarriages of their government. If it were not true, it is very strange, that two such great *Apostles*, should use such an argument to perswade Christians to submit to the powers, as only proved the quite contrary, that they ought not to be subject to the present powers, because they were unjust and Tyrannical, and in contradiction to the original design and institution of civil power, were a terror to good works and not to the evil.

The *Christians* were at that time persecuted by *Jews* and *Heathens*, by all the powers of the World. The Apostle exhorts them not to resist the powers, because they were not a Terror to good works, but to the evil. If by this he only means, that they should be subject to them, while they encouraged Vertue and vertuous men, but might rebel against them, when they did the contrary; how could the *Christians* of those days

days think themselves obliged by this to submit to the higher powers?

For this was not their case. They suffered for righteousness sake; the powers were a terrour to them, though they were innocent, though they could not charge them, either with breaking the Laws of God or Men; and therefore they were not bound to submit to them, whenever they could find it safe to resist. So that either these men put a false comment upon the Text, or while the *Apostle* undertakes to deter them from resistance, he urges such an argument as was proper only to perswade them to rebel.

2. We may also consider, that this interpretation of the words makes the Apostles argument childish and ludicrous, and wholly useless to perswade any man to be subject, who needs perswasion. For I take it for granted, that there is no need to perswade any man, especially the good and vertuous, not to resist the powers, when he meets with the just rewards and encouragements of Vertue. The usual pretence for seditions and Treasons, is to redress publick grievances, to deliver themselves from a state of oppression and slavery; but all

mankind agree, that they ought to obey Governours, who govern well; and no man thinks it juſt or honourable to rebel, who has not, or cannot pretend ſome cauſe of complaint. The tryal of our obedience is, when we ſuffer injuriouſly for righteouſneſs ſake, when our Rights and Liberties are invaded, when we groan under ſuch oppreſſions, as are enough to make a *wiſe man mad*, and to tranſport him to irregular and unjuſtifiable actions. This was the caſe of the Primitive Chriſtians to whom the Apoſtles wrote, and therefore we might reaſonably expect, that he ſhould urge ſuch Arguments to Subjection, as ſhould reach their caſe: but if theſe men be good Expoſitors, the Apoſtle ſays nothing to perſwade any man to obedience to the powers, who finds the powers uneaſie and troubleſome to him; and thoſe who have nothing to *complain* of, one would think, ſhould need no Arguments to perſwade them to ſubjection to ſo eaſie and gentle a yoak.

3. Nay, according to this interpretation of the Doctrine of *Subjection*, that we are bound only to be ſubject to thoſe *Princes*, who rule well, who puniſh wickedneſs and reward vertue; this Doctrine

of

of *Subjection* gives no security at all to the best governments in the world. The most Factious and Seditious spirits can desire no greater liberty, than this principle grants them. For no humane government can be so exact and perfect, but it may be guilty of great miscarriages. Good men may suffer, and bad men may flourish under a vertuous *Prince*, and therefore ill designing men can never want pretences to misrepresent the government, and to foment Discontents and Jealousies between Prince and People. This unhappy Nation has been a sad example of this, twice in one Age, under two as *just* and *merciful Princes*, as ever sate upon the English Throne. When there were never fewer real grievances to be complained of, and never more loud and Tragical complaints: and if Subjects are not bound to obey any longer than all things please and gratifie their humors, it is a vain thing to name the Doctrine of *Subjection*; which is of no use at all to the peace and security of humane Societies.

4. This is absolutely false, that we are bound to be subject to *Soveraign Princes* no longer than they rule well, according to the measures of Justice and

and righteousness. The Apostle I am sure supposes the contrary, when he tells the Christians, *But and if ye suffer for righteousness sake, happy are ye; and be not afraid of their terror, neither be troubled,* 1 Pet. 3. 14. Thus he commands servants *to be subject to their Masters with fear, not only to the good and gentle, but also to the froward. For this is thankworthy, if a man for conscience towards God endure grief, suffering patiently. For what glory is it, if when ye be buffeted for your faults, ye take it patiently? but if when ye do well and suffer for it, ye take it patiently, this is acceptable with God,* 2 *Chap.* 18, 19, 20. And certainly there is as perfect a subjection due to a *Soverain Prince* as to a *Master*, for he is more eminently the Minister of God, and acts by a more Sacred and inviolable authority. And that this does extend to our subjection to *Princes*, appears from the example of Christ, which the Apostle there recommends to our imitation, who was the most innocent person in the world, and yet suffered the most barbarous usage, not from the hands of a private Master, but of the supreme powers. And therefore when he commands in the same Chapter to sub-

submit to Governours, *as to those who are for the punishment of evil doers, and the praise of them that do well*, it is evident, that he did not intend this as a limitation of our subjection, as if we were not bound to be subject in other cases; since, in the very same Chapter, he requires subjection not only to the *good and gentle*, *but also to the froward*, in imitation of the example of our Lord, who suffered patiently under unjust and Tyrannical powers.

5. I observe therefore, that the Apostle does not alleadge this as the reason of our subjection, but as a motive or argument to reconcile us to the practice of it. The reason of our subjection to *Princes* is, that they are advanced by God, that they are his Ministers, that those *who resist, resist the Ordinance of God*, and therefore *we must submit for Gods sake*, out of reverence to his authority. But it is an encouragement to subjection, to consider the great advantages of government, that *Rulers are not a terrour to good works, but to the evil.* But though this motive should fail in some instances, yet while the reason of subjection lasts, (and that can never fail, while we own the Soverain Authority of God) so long it is

our

our dutie to be subject, whether our *Prince* do his dutie or not.

6. But to examine more particularly the meaning of these words. When the Apostle says, that *Rulers are not a terror to good works, but to the evil ; that they are for the punishment of evil doers, and the praise of them that do well* ; I see no necessitie of expounding this of good and evil works in general, that all good and virtuous actions shall be rewarded by them, and all evil actions punish't ; for this is almost impossible in any humane government; and there never was any government in the world, that appointed rewards for all virtuous actions, and punishments for all wicked ones. But these good and evil works seem to be confined to the matter in hand, to subjection and obedience, as a good and virtuous action. And so the Apostle enforces this dutie of subjection, not onely from the Authoritie of God, but from the power of Princes: *Be subject to the higher powers; for Rulers are not a terrour to good works, but to the evil.* We need not fear the powers, when we obey them, and submit ourselves to them; but they will punish us if we rebel. The force of which argument is this:

The

The best way to obtain safetie and protection under any Government, is by being peaceable, quiet, and obedient; such men generally escape under the greatest *Tyrants*; for *Tyrants* themselves do not use to insult over the peaceable and obedient: but if men be seditious and troublesome to government, then *he beareth not the sword in vain, but is the Minister of God, a revenger to execute wrath upon him that doeth evil*, that is, upon all disobedience and rebellion; for whatever wickedness escapes unpunish't, Princes for their own securitie must not suffer disobedience and rebellion to escape. And that this is the meaning of it, appears from the next verse, where the *Apostle* sums up the whole argument for subjection, which he reduces to *Conscience towards God, and fear* of the secular powers: *Wherefore ye must needs be subject, not onely for wrath, but also for Conscience sake*. And that St. *Peter* by well doing means subjection to *Princes*, is very plain. *For so is the will of God, that with well doing, ye should put to silence the ignorance of foolish men*; that is, by obedience and subjection to *Princes*, which is the dutie he there exhorts them to. And therefore it is very probable that

that he means the same by *well doing* in the verse before, that Governours are for the *punishment of evil* doers, *and the praise of them that do well*; to punish the disobedient and rebellious, and to reward and protect those, who live in all quiet and peaceable subjection. And if this be the meaning of it, I think they can find no limitation here of our *subjection to Princes*.

7. But let us suppose, that when the *Apostle* says, that *Rulers are not a terror to good works, but to the evil*, he understands by it in general, the great advantages of civil government, that is, for the suppression of wickedness, and incouragement of virtue, which is the true end and the best improvement of humane power; this also is in a great measure true of the worst and most Tyrannical Princes, and therefore the argument for subjection is good even under a Tyrant.

Publick Justice was administred under the government of *Nero*, and good men were rewarded, and bad men punish't: And though Justice be not so equally and so universally administred under a *bad Prince*, as under a *good* one; though a Tyrant may oppress many of his

his subjects, and be the occasion of great Calamities, yet while there is any publick government maintained in the world, it lays great restraints upon the unruly lusts and passions of men, and gives great securitie to the just and innocent. And therefore good men are concerned to promote the peace and securitie of Government, though the Prince be a Tyrant: for there is more Justice to be had under a *Tyrant*, than in a civil War. In ordinary cases it is very possible for good men to live easily and tolerably under a very *bad Prince*; & though it should be their lot to suffer, yet since the peace and quiet of humane Societies is in it self so great a blessing, and the publick good is better consulted by the preservation of government, than by resistance, it becomes every good man rather to suffer patiently under a *Tyrant*, than to shake and unsettle humane government, and disturb the natural course of Justice by seditions and tumults.

8. Nay let us suppose, that the Apostle here speaks of such an equal administration of Justice, as cannot be expected under the government of a *Tyrant*; yet so the argument holds good against resistance, though our *Prince* be
never

never so bad. And it lies thus: we must not resist the powers, because *Rulers are not a terrour to good works, but to the evil.* This is the great blessing of humane government, to preserve Justice and righteousness among men. For this reason God has intrusted the *Princes* with the power of the sword, for *the punishment of evil doers, and the praise of them that do well*; and therefore we must not resist him, because publick Justice is so great a blessing to the world. But how does this follow, you will say, that we must not resist a Tyrant, who is so far from administring Justice, that he oppresses his subjects, because Civil Government and Publick Justice is so great a blessing? what agreement is there between civil government, and publick Justice and a Tyrant? Why the consequence is very plain. Civil government, which is for the administration of publick Justice, is a great and inestimable blessing to the world: but now there can be no civil government without a supreme and irresistible power; publick Justice cannot be administred, unless there is some power from whence there is no appeal. It is not necessarie indeed, that the power

power should always be in the hands of one man: but if God have placed this power in the hands of a *Prince*, there it must be irresistible too, however he uses it: for if once it be made lawful to resist the supreme Power, wherever it is plac't, you dissolve humane Societies, or at least expose them to perpetual disorders and convulsions. Factious and ambitious men will find pretences to resist good Princes as well as the bad, and no government can be any longer secure, than while ill-designing men want power to resist. Now then, to pass a true Judgement of this matter, we must not onely consider, what present inconveniencies we may suffer from the irresistible power of a *Tyrant*, but what an irreparable mischief it is for ever to unsettle the foundations of government. We must consider whether Civil Government be the greater blessing to mankind, or a *Tyrant* the greater curse: whether it be more desirable to endure the insolence and injustice of a *Tyrant*, when the power falls into such a hand; or for ever to be deprived of the securitie of government, and the blessings of Peace and order. And therefore there is great reason, why God should

M so

so severely forbid the resistance of *Princes*, though *Tyrants*; and why we should quietly and contentedly submit to this divine appointment, because the resistance of the supreme power, were it once allowed by God, would weaken the authoritie of humane Governments, and expose them to the rage and frenzie of ambitious and discontented *Statesmen*, or wild *Enthusiasts*. This I think is a sufficient answer to this pretence, that the Apostle limits our subjection to Princes to the regular exercise of their authoritie.

3. It is objected also from St. *Peters* words, that the inferiour and subordinate Magistrates receive their power from God also, as well as *supreme* and *Soveraign Princes*; Governours are sent *by him*, that is, say they, by God, for *the punishment of evil doers, and the praise of them that do well*; and therefore though private men may not resist a *Soveraign Prince*, yet publick Magistrates may, though they be not supreme; for it is their dutie also to see wickedness punish't, and virtue rewarded; and therefore it is part of their *Commission* to give check to the Soveraign Power, and to defend subjects from the
un-

unjust violence and oppressions of their *Prince*. And this the *Emperour Trajan* learn't from the common principles of Justice and Equitie, who delivered a sword to one of his Officers with this charge, to use it for him, while he governed well, but against him if he governed ill. Now in answer to this, we may consider,

1. That there is no foundation at all for this in the *Text*, for this δι αὐτῶ or *by him*, cannot by any rules of Grammar be referred to God, but to the *King*. *Submit to every Ordinance of man for the Lord's sake, whether to the King as supreme, or unto Governours, as unto them who are sent by him.* *By him?* by whom? by God? that is not said, but by the *King*, for that is the next antecedent; and that is the evident truth of the case. Inferiour Magistrates do not receive their power from *God*, but from the *King*, who having the Soveraign power in himself, commits the exercise of some part of it to others, and taketh it away again, when he pleases. And the very phrase of πεμπομένοις δι αὐτῶ, those who are sent by him, plainly refers it to those who were sent by the *Emperour* into forreign countries, to go-

vern the *Roman Provinces*; such as *Pontius Pilate* and *Felix* were: and so the meaning is, that they were not onely obliged to submit to the *Roman Emperours*, but to all those Governours, whom they sent to rule the Provinces under their Jurisdiction; which is no more than for a Preacher to instruct the subjects of *Ireland*, that they must not onely submit to the King, but to all those whom he sent to govern them, with the power and authoritie of *Deputies*, or *Lord-Lieutenants*.

2. Nay St. *Peter*, as if he had foreseen this objection, takes particular care to prevent it, and therefore makes an apparent difference between that submission we owe to *Soveraign Princes*, and that which we owe to Governours; we must submit *to the King as supreme*, ὡς ὑπερέχοντι as to him who is above all, whose power is unaccountable and irresistible; but *to Governours, as unto them who are sent by him:* which both signifies the reason of our submission to Governours, and prescribes the bounds and measures of it.

The reason why we must submit to *Governours*, is because they are sent by our *Prince*, they act by his Authoritie, and

and therefore we must submit to, and reverence his Authoritie in them. It is not for their own sakes, nor for any inherent Authoritie in them, but as they receive their power from our *Prince*.

And this also determines the bounds and measures of our subjection to Governours. As that Authoritie, which they receive from the *King*, is the onely reason why we must submit to them at all: so we must submit no longer, than that Authoritie lasts; when ever the *Prince* recalls them, and transfers this power to another, we must obey them no longer. Nay, since we are onely bound to reverence and obey the authoritie of our *Prince* in them, we must never submit to them in opposition to our *Prince*. Our primarie obligation is to submit to the *King*, who is our *Soveraign Lord*, and must in no cases be resisted; our submission to Governours and subordinate Magistrates is onely a part and branch of our dutie to the *King*, as they are his Officers and Ministers: and therefore it can never be our dutie to obey or comply with subordinate Magistrates, but onely when it is an act of dutie and subjection to our *Prince*; and certainly it is no act of subjection to our *Prince* to obey subordinate Magistrates, when they rebel against their *Prince*: for, to resist a *Prince*, or to joyn with those who do resist him, is an odde kind of instance of our subjection to him. This is not to submit to the *King a Supreme, nor to Governours, as unto those who are sent by him*, and receive their Authoritie from him: but it is to submit to Governours, as the supreme and soveraign *Judges* of our *Prince*, and the *Patrons* and *Protectors* of the *people* against their *Prince*: which is directly contrarie to St. *Peter's* Doctrine.

It was no new thing for the Governours of remote *Provinces* to revolt from the obedience of the *Roman Emperours*, and to usurp a Soveraign and Imperial Authoritie to themselves; and therefore St. *Peter* expresses their dutie to Governours with this caution and limitation, that though they must submit to those, whom the Emperour sent to govern them, yet it must be in subordination to the Imperial Authoritie, and with a reserve of that more absolute subjection, which they owe to the *Emperour* himself, who is their *Soveraign Lord*. While Governours are subject to the *Emperour*, who is their Lord and Master, ther, we must be subject to them: but if they rebel, we must be subject to the *Emperour* still, and oppose those, whom we were before bound to obey.

When St. *Peter* so expresly commands them both to submit to the *King*, and to submit to Governours, it is impossible he could consider the *King* and Governours, as two distinct and rival authorities; for then it might so happen, that they could not submit to both, if ever they should oppose each other: and therefore when he commands them to submit to both, he must suppose them to be both one, as the fountain and the stream is one. The Authority to which they must submit is but one, it is originally in the *King*, as in its source and fountain, and it is derived and communicated to Governours: but is the same power still, which as necessarily depends upon the *King*, as light does upon the Sun; and therefore when these powers grow two, when this derivative and dependant power sets up for it self in opposition to that power which gave it its being, we are delivered from our subjection to it, because it ceases to be one with that soveraign power, to which we must be subject.

Once

Once more. St. *Peter* commands the Christians to submit to the *King*, and to *Governours*, that is, to the King's Ministers, who receive their authority from him to govern. But when such persons rebel against their *Prince* who gave them authority, they cease to be the Kings Ministers and Governours, and therefore cease to be such Governours to whom the Apostle commands submission. We are to obey them while they are the *Kings* Ministers and Deputies; but when they assume to themselves an independant power, we must submit to them no longer, but to our *Prince*: We may and ought to obey our *Prince*, and those Magistrates whom he sets over us, but we cannot submit to our *Prince* and to *Rebels*; and certainly when men become *Rebels*, they are no longer the *Kings* Ministers, but his *Rivals*.

3. It is a very ridiculous pretence also, which has no foundation in St. *Peter*'s words, that Governours or subordinate Magistrates have power to controul or resist their *Soverain Prince*. The Apostle tells us, that the King is supreme; but over whom is he supreme? certainly over all in his Dominions, or else he is not supreme; and therefore he

is

is supreme with respect to subordinate Magistrates, as well as private Subjects; and then they have no more power or authority to resist, than any private Subject has. For St. *Paul* tells us, the *higher Power* is irresistible; which would be a strange Paradox, if every little Officer had authority to resist him.

And yet if men will grant, that it is never lawful for any private man to resist his *Prince,* it is not worth disputing, whether subordinate Magistrates may or not; for if private men must not resist, these inferiour Magistrates cannot, or at least they will resist to no purpose. He may make them private men again when he pleases; or however, he must be an *unfortunate Prince,* whom all his own Officers and Ministers conspire against; and he must be a very *weak Prince,* who has not force and power to oppose them. For what does the discontent of the greatest *Ministers* signifie, who can raise no forces to oppose their *Prince?* and yet there are no forces to be raised, if private men must not resist. When inferiour Magistrates must submit, or rebel alone, (as they must do, if private men must not rebel) whatever
autho-

authority they have to controul their Prince, they will want force and power to do it. And yet it would be a lewd way of burlesquing this Doctrine of *Non-resistance*, to make no more of it than this, that when St. *Paul* so severely threatens damnation against those who resist, his meaning is, that private Subjects must not resist their Prince, unless they have some discontented and factious Magistrates to head them.

But how should these *subordinate Governours* come by this power to resist their *Prince*? They must either have it from God, or from their *Prince*. Not from *God*. For *Soverain Princes* receive their authority from God; and if God have bestowed the supreme and Soverain Power on the *Prince*, it is a contradiction to say, that he has advanced his own Ministers and Officers above him; which would be to place a superiour power over the supreme. Nor is it reasonable to suppose, that inferiour Magistrates receive such a power as this from their *Prince*, though it is evident, they have no power, but what they receive from him. For notwithstanding *Trajan*'s complement, which he never intended should be made a Law for himself,

self, or other Soverain Princes; no Prince can give such power as this to a Subject, without giving him his Crown. He gives away his Soverain power, when he gives any Subject authority to resist; he ceases to be a *Soverain Prince*, if he makes any man his Superior: for he cannot give away Soverain power, and yet keep it himself. And it would be a hard case with *Princes*, had they as many Judges and Masters, as they have Officers and Ministers of State. Indeed, no *Prince* without parting with his Crown, can grant such an extravagant power to any Subject: for while he continues Soverain, God has made it necessary to the greatest Subjects to obey and submit. For as for *Trajan's* saying to one of his Commanders, when he delivered him the Sword, *Use this for me if I govern well, and against me if I govern ill*, it only signified his fixt resolution to govern well, and that he would imploy it in no ill services: but it conveyed no more power to him to rebel, if he should govern ill, than a Father's saying to his Son, that he should forgive his disobedience, if ever he would prove unkind, would justifie the disobedience of the Son, if his Father should prove un-

unkind. The duties of these relations are fixt by God, and cannot be altered by men. A *Prince* may divest himself of his Kingdom, and royal Power; but while he continues Soveraign, he cannot give liberty to any man to resist him.

4. There is another objection not onely to invalidate St. *Peters* authoritie, but to answer all the arguments that are produced from the doctrine and practice of Christ and his Apostles, to inforce this dutie of Non-resistance and subjection to Princes; and that is, that these commands were onely temporarie, and obliged Christians while they wanted force and power to resist, but do not oblige us, when we can resist and conquer too.

I have sometimes thought, that this objection ought to be answered onely with indignation and abhorrence, as an open contempt of the authoritie of the Scriptures, and blasphemie against the holy Spirit, by which they were indited; but it may be, it is better to answer and expose it, and let the world see, besides the notorious folly of it, how near a kin the doctrine of Resistance is to Atheism, Infidelity, and Blasphemy.

1.

1. First then I observe, that this very objection supposes that the doctrine of the Gospel is against Resistance; for those who evade the authoritie of the Scriptures, by saying, that Christians were then forbid to resist, because they wanted power to conquer, must grant, that resistance is forbid. Which is a plain confession, that they are conscious to themselves, that all the arts they have us'd to make the Scriptures speak their sence, and justifie the Doctrine of Resistance, will not do. And therefore when men are once reduced to this last refuge, to confess, that the Scriptures are against them, if they have any modesty left, they ought never to pretend to the authority of the Scriptures in this cause more. And this is a sufficient answer to all men, who have any reverence for the authority of the Scriptures, that they cannot resist their *Prince* without disobeying the plain and express Laws of the Gospel; for he is a bold man, who will venture his eternal Salvation, upon pleading his exemption from any express Law.

2. I would desire all men who have any reverence left for the Religion of our Saviour, to consider seriously how
this

this pretence does disparage and weaken the authority of the Gospel, and make it a very imperfect, and a very uncertain rule of Life, which every man may fit and accommodate to his own humour and inclinations.

Christ and his Apostles do in the most express terms, and under the most severe penalties, forbid the resistance of Soveraign Princes. But say these men, this law does not oblige us now, though it did oblige the Christians of those days; for our circumstances are much changed and altered. The Christians at that time were weak, and unable to resist, and therefore were taught to suffer patiently without resistance; but thanks be to God, the case is not thus now; and therefore we may vindicate our natural and religious rights and liberties against all unjust violence. Now observe what follows from hence:

1. That the Gospel of our Saviour is a very imperfect and uncertain rule of life; that it absolutely forbids things, which are not absolutely evil, but sometimes lawful, without allowing for such a difference: that it gives general laws, which oblige onely at certain times, or in some circumstances, without giving any

any notice in what cafes they do not oblige; which is a mightie fnare to mens confciences, or a great injury to their Chriftian libertie. It impofes this hard neceffitie upon them, either to make bold with a divine law, if they do refift Tyrannical powers, which is grievous to a tender confcience, which has any reverence for God; or to fuffer injurioufly, when they need not, had they been plainly inftructed in their dutie, and acquainted in what cafes they might refift, and in what not. And I think, there cannot be a greater reproach to the Gofpel, than to make it fuch an imperfect and infnaring rule.

2. Nay, this charges Chrift and his Apoftles with want of finceritie in preaching the Gofpel; for either they knew, that this Doctrine of *Non-refiftance* did not oblige all Chriftians, but onely thofe who are weak and unable to refift, or they did not. If we fay they did not, we charge them with ignorance; if we fay they did, with difhoneftie: for if they knew, that all Chriftians were not obliged to fuch an abfolute fubjection to *Princes*, as in no cafe to refift, why did they conceal fo important a truth, without giving the leaft
in-

intimation of it? Did they think this so scandalous a Doctrine, that they were afraid or ashamed to publish it to the world? and can any thing be a Doctrine of the Gospel, which is truly scandalous? But was the Doctrine of *resistance* more scandalous, than the Doctrine of the *Cross*? Would this have offended *Princes*, and make them more implacable enemies to Christianitie? But would it not also have made more converts? would not a libertie to resist the powers, and defend themselves, been a better inducement to imbrace Christianitie, than a necessitie of suffering the worst things for the Name of Christ? would not this have contributed very much to the conversion of the whole *Jewish Nation*, who were fond of a *Temporal Kingdom*, had Christianitie allowed them to cast off the *Roman Yoke*, and restored their ancient liberties? How soon should we have seen the *Cross* in their *Banners*, and how gladly would they have fought under that victorious signe, under the conduct of so many wonder-working Prophets? and how soon would this have made the Doctrine of *Non-resistance* useless and out of date, by making Christians powerful enough

enough to refift? So that there is no imaginable reafon, why Chrift and his Apoftle fhould conceal this Doctrine of the lawfulnefs of refifting perfecuting and Tyrannical powers, efpecially at that time, when if it had been lawful, there was as much ufe for it, and as great reafon to preach it, as ever there was, or ever can be. And therefore we muft either think very ill of our Saviour and his Apoftles, or acknowledge, that this is no Gofpel-Doctrine, never was, and never can be any part of the Religion of the Crofs. There is no reafon, why Chrift fhould at firft plant Chriftianity in the world by fufferings, if it might afterwards be maintained and propagated by glorious rebellions.

3. If this plea be allowed, it weakens the Authoritie of all the laws of the Gofpel, and leaves men at libertie to difpence with themfelves, when they fee or fancie any reafon for it. *Non-refiftance* is as abfolutely commanded, as any other law of the Gofpel; but thefe men imagine, without any other reafon, but becaufe they would have it fo, that this law onely concerned Chriftians in the weak and Infant-ftate of the Church, while they were unable to refift. Now fhou'd other

ther men take the same libertie with other laws (and I know no reason but why they may) how easie were it to expound Christianitie out of the world? Meekness, patience, humilitie, selfdenial, contempt of the world, forgiving enemies, contentment in all conditions, are parts and branches of this suffering Religion; and may we not with as much reason say, that these duties were calculated for the afflicted and suffering state of the Church, when the profession of Christianitie was discouraged in the world, and exposed them to the loss of all things, and therefore made it impossible for them to enjoy those pleasures and advantages of life, which other men did; but that they do not more oblige us than resistance, now the Church is flourishing and prosperous? And thus men may justifie their pride and ambition and covetousness, and may be as very Idolaters of the riches and pleasures and honours of the world, as Heathens themselves, when Christianity became the Religion of the Empire: it did indeed make too great an alteration in the lives of Christians. But according to this way of reasoning, it made as great an alteration in Religion it self; at this rate we ought

ought to have two Gospels, one for the afflicted, the other for the prosperous state of the Church; which differ as much as *Christianity* and *Paganism* in the great rules of life. But we are hard dealt with, that we have but one Gospel, and that the Suffering Gospel; and for my part, I dare not undertake to make another. So that this plea for resistance in opposition to the plain and express Laws of the Gospel, in the consequences of it, strikes at the very foundations of Christianitie, and becomes the mouth of none but an *Atheist* or an *Infidel*.

4. This is a very absurd pretence, that the Apostle forbids the Christians of those days to resist, onely because they were weak, and unable to resist. This is a great reproach to the Apostle, as if he were of the temper of some men, who crouch and flatter, and pretend great loyaltie, when they are afraid to rebel, but are loyal no longer than they have an opportunitie to rebel. This is dissimulation and flatterie, and inconsistent with the open simplicitie of the Apostolick Spirit; but it is very strange that the Apostle should so severely forbid resistance, when he knew they could not resist. One would think common Prudence

Prudence should teach such men to be quiet and Subject; and therefore his zeal and vehemence would perswade one, that as weak as the Christians were, yet in those days they could have resisted. Nay, it is evident, that there were a sort of men who in those days called themselves Christians, and yet did resist the powers; such were the *Gnostick Hereticks,* who *despised Government,* who were *presumptuous and selfwilled,* and were *not afraid to speak evil of dignities*, 2. Peter 2. 10. Jude v. 8. for to reproach and vilifie Government, is one degree of resistance; and no men are so weak, but they may do that. Nay, though Christians had not power enough of their own to have rebelled against the *Roman Government,* yet they had opportunitie enough to joyn and conspire with those who had, and to have made good terms and conditions for themselves. They lived in a very factious age, when both Jews and Heathens were very apt to rebel, and could both have promoted and strengthned the Faction, if they had pleased, and have grown very acceptable to them by doing so; and though no man knows what the event of any rebellion will be,

till

till he tries, yet they might have escaped as well as other men. This the Apostle knew, and this he was afraid of, and this he warns them against; and that for such reasons, as plainly shew, that it was not a meer prudential advice he gives them, for that time, but a standing Law of their Religion.

5. For this Doctrine of *Non-resistance* is urged with such reasons and arguments, as are good in all ages of the Church, as well when Christians have power to resist and conquer, as when they have not. Thus (1.) St. *Paul* inforces this dutie of subjection to the *Higher powers*, because *all powers are of God; the powers that be are ordained of God;* and therefore *he that resisteth the powers, resisteth the Ordinance of God.* Now if they must obey the powers, because they are from God, *Subjection* and *Non-resistance* is as much our dutie, when we have power to resist, as when we have not; and is as much our dutie at this day, as it was in the time of the Apostle, if we believe, that God has as great a hand in setting up Kings now, as he had then.

2. He threatens eternal damnation against those, who resist: *He that resists*

shall receive unto himself damnation; which supposes, that there is a moral evil in resistance, and therefore that Non-resistance is an eternal and unchangeable Law: which cannot be true, if it be lawful to resist, when we can resist to some purpose, when we can resist and conquer. It is foolish indeed to resist a *Prince*, when we have not sufficient force to oppose against him; but it would be a hard case, if a man should perish etenally, for doing an action, which is lawful in it self, but imprudently undertaken. These men had need look well to themselves, how lawful soever they think resistance to be, if every imprudent and unfortunate Rebel must be damned.

3. St. *Paul* addes, that *we must needs be subject, not onely for wrath, but also for Conscience sake*; that is, not onely out of fear of men, but out of Conscience of our dutie to God. Now if resistance were not in its nature sinful, it were a very prudential Consideration, not to resist for fear of wrath, that is, for fear of being punish't by men, if we cannot conquer; but there would be no conscience in the case, no sence of any dutie to God: unless we think, that *Non-resistance* is our dutie,

duty, when we cannot conquer, and resistance when we can.

4. St. *Peter* tells us, that this subjection to Kings and Governours is a good and vertuous action, and therefore he calls it *well-doing: For so is the will of God, that with well-doing ye may put to silence the ignorance of foolish men*; that is, by submitting to *Kings* and *Governours*, as you have already heard. Now the nature of Vertue and Vice cannot alter with the circumstances of our condition; that which is good in one age, is so in another; which shews, that *Subjection* and *Non-resistance* was not a temporary law, and meer matter of prudence, but an essential duty of Christian Religion.

5. For it appears by what he adds, that it was a great credit and reputation to Christianity, that it made men quiet, peaceable, and governable; *By well-doing they put to silence the ignorance of foolish men*; by their peaceable and obedient behaviour to their Governours, they sham'd those men, who ignorantly reproach't the Christian Religion. Now hence there are two plain consequents:

1. That subjection to government is a thing of very good repute in the world,

or else it could be no Credit to Christianity; and this is a good argument that subjection to Government is a great Vertue, because all men speak well of it. It is a thing of *good report*, and therefore becomes Christians, 4 *Phil.* 8.

2. It hence follows also, that subjection to Government was a standing Doctrine of the Christian Religion, because it was the will of God, that they should recommend Christianity to the world by *subjection* to *Princes*. But certainly God never intended they should put a cheat upon the world, and recommend Christianity to them, by that, which is no part nor duty of Christianity.

This is abundantly sufficient to confute that vain pretence, that the Doctrine of *Subjection* and *Non-resistance* obliged Christians only, while they were unable to resist and defend themselves; and this is enough to satisfie us, what the Doctrine of the Apostles was about subjection to *Princes*.

As for their examples, I think there was never any dispute about that. It is sufficiently known, that they suffered Martyrdom, as a vast number of Christians in that and some following Ages did, without either reproaching their Gover-

Governours, or rebelling against them: and this they did, as they taught others to do, not meerly because they could not resist, but out of duty and reverence to God, who sets Princes on Thrones, and has given them a sacred and inviolable Authority; and in imitation of their great Lord and Master, who went as a Lamb to the slaughter, and as a sheep before the shearer is dumb, so he opened not his mouth.

CHAP.

CHAP. VI.

An ANSWER *to the most Popular Objections against* NON-RESISTANCE.

I Proceed now to consider those objections, which are made against the Doctrine of *Non-resistance*; though methinks after such plain and convincing proof, that *Non-resistance* is the Doctrine both of the Old and New Testament, though witty men may be able to start some objections, yet wise and good men should not regard them: for no objection is of any force, against a plain and express Law of God. Indeed, when we have no evidence for a thing but only Natural Reason, and the reason seems to be equally strong and cogent on both sides, it renders the matter very doubtful, on which side the truth lies: but when on one side there is a plain and express *Revelation* of the will of God, and on the other side some shew and appearance of reason, I think there can be no dispute

dispute, which side we chuse; unless any man think it doubtful, which is the most certain and infallible rule. *Scripture* or *meer natural reason*. And therefore till men can answer that Scripture-evidence, which I have produced, (which I am not much concerned about, for I guess it will take them up some time to do it) all their other objections, whether I could answer them or not, signifie nothing at all to me, and ought to signifie as little to any man, who reverences the Scriptures. But let us consider their objections; for they are not so formidable, that we need be afraid of them.

Now I know no body, but will acknowledge, that in most cases it is the duty of Subjects not to resist their *Prince*; but they only pretend, that this is not their duty, when their *Prince* oppresses and persecutes them contrary to Law: when their Lives and Liberties and Properties and Religion are all secured by the Laws of the Land, they see no reason why they should tamely suffer a *Prince* to usurp upon them, why they should not defend themselves against all unjust and illegal violence; and they urge several arguments to prove, that they may do so; which may be reduced to these five.   1. That

1. That they are bound by no Law to suffer against Law. 2. That the Prince has no authority against Law. 3. That they have a natural right of self-defence against unjust violence. 4. That otherwise we destroy the distinction between an *absolute* and *limited* Monarch; between a *Prince* whose *will is his Law*, and a *Prince* who is bound to govern by Law; which undermines the Fundamental Constitution of the English Government. 5. That if resistance in no case be allowed, the mischiefs and inconveniencies to mankind may be intolerable. I suppose it will be acknowledged, that these five particulars do contain the whole strength of their cause; and if I can give a fair answer to them, it must either make men Loyal, or leave them without excuse.

1. They urge, that they are bound by no Law to suffer against Law. Suppose, as a late Author does, that a Popish Prince should persecute his Protestant Subjects in *England* for professing the Protestant Religion which is established by Law; *By what Law* (saies he) *must we die? not by any Law of God surely, for being of that Religion, which he approves,*

Julian the Apostate.

proves, and would have all the world to embrace, and to hold fast to the end. Nor by the Laws of our Country, where Protestancy is so far from being criminal, that it is death to desert it, and to turn *Papist*. By what Law then ? by none that *I know of*, saies our *Author* : nor do I know of any ; and so far we are agreed. But then both the Laws of God and of our Countrie, command us not to resist : and if death, an illegal unjust death follow upon that, I cannot help it ; God and our Countrie must answer for it. It is a wonderful discoverie, which this *Author* has made, that when we suffer against Law, we are condemned by no Law to die ; for if we were, we could not suffer against Law : and it is as wonderful an argument he uses to prove, that we may resist, when we are persecuted against Law, because we are condemned by no Law to die ; which is supposed in the very question, and is neither more nor less, than to affirm the thing which he was to prove. We may resist a Prince who persecutes against Law, because we are condemned by no Law, that is, because he persecutes against Law. This proves indeed, that we ought not to die, when we are condemned by no Law to die,

die; but whether we may preserve our selves from an unjust and violent death by resisting a persecuting Prince, is another question.

2. It is urged, that a Prince has no authoritie against Law; *There is no authority on earth above the Law, much less against it. It is Murder to put a man to death against Law; and if they knew who had authority to commit open, bare-faced, and downright Murders, this would direct them where to pay their Passive Obedience; but it would be the horridest slander in the world to say, that any such power is lodged in the Prerogative, as to destroy men contrary to Law.*

Now I perfectly agree with them in this also, that a *Prince* has no just and legal authoritie to act against Law; that if he knowingly persecute any Subject to death contrary to Law, he is a Murderer, and that no *Prince* has any such *Prerogative* to commit *open, bare-faced and downright murders.* But what follows from hence? does it hence follow, therefore we may resist and oppose them, if they do? This I absolutely denie; because God has expresly commanded us not to resist: And I see no inconsistencie between these two propositions

sitions, that a *Prince* has no Legal Authoritie to persecute against Law, and yet that he must not be resisted, when he does. Both the Laws of God, and the Laws of our Countrie, suppose these two to be very consistent. For notwithstanding the possibilitie, that *Princes* may abuse their power, and transgress the Laws, whereby they ought to govern; yet they Command Subjects in no case to resist: and it is not sufficient to justifie resistance, if Princes do, what they have no just Authoritie to do, unless we have also a just Authoritie to resist. He, who exceeds the just bounds of his Authoritie, is lyable to be called to an account for it; but he is accountable onely to those, who have a superior authoritie to call him to an account. No power whatever is accountable to an inferiour; for this is a contradiction to the very notion of Power, and destructive of all Order and Government. Inferiour Magistrates are on all hands acknowledged to be lyable to give an account of the abuse of their power; but to whom must they give an account? not to their inferiours; not to the people, whom they are to Govern, but to superiour Magistrates, or to the *Soveraign*

raign Prince, who governs all. Thus the *Soveraign Prince* may exceed his Authoritie, and is accountable for it to a superiour power; but because he has no superiour power on earth, he cannot be resisted by his own Subjects, but must be reserved to the Judgement of God, who alone is the *King of Kings*. To justifie our resistance of any power, there are two things to be proved. 1. That this power has exceeded its just Authoritie. 2. That we have Authoritie to resist. Now these men indeed prove the first very well, that *Princes*, who are to govern by Law, exceed their legal Authoritie when they persecute against Law: but they say not one word of the second, that Subjects have authoritie to resist their *Prince*, who persecutes against Law; which was the onely thing, that needed proof: but this is a hard task, and therefore they thought it more adviseable to take it for granted, than to attempt to prove it. They say indeed, *that an inauthoritative act, which carries no obligation at all, cannot oblige Subjects to obedience.* Now this is manifestly true, if by obedience they mean an *active obedience*; for I am not bound to do an ill thing, or an illegal action, because my my *Prince* commands me; but if they mean *Passive Obedience*, it is as manifestly false; for I am bound to obey, that is, not to resist my *Prince*, when he offers the most unjust and illegal violence.

Nay, it is very false and absurd to say, that every illegal, is an inauthoritative act, which carries no obligation with it. This is contrarie to the practice of all *humane Judicatures*, and the daily experience of men, who suffer in their lives, bodies, or estates by an unjust and illegal sentence. Every Judgement contrarie to the true meaning of the law, is in that sence illegal; and yet such illegal Judgements have their Authoritie and obligation, till they are rescinded by some higher Authoritie. This is the true reason of appeals from inferiour to superiour Courts, to rectifie illegal proceedings, and reverse illegal Judgements; which supposes that such illegal acts have authoritie, till they are made null and void by a higher power: and if the higher powers from whence lies no appeal, confirm and ratifie an unjust and illegal sentence, it carries so much authoritie and obligation with it, that the injured person has no redress, but must patiently

tiently submit; and thus it must necessarily be, or there can be no end of disputes, nor any order and Government in humane Societies.

And this is a plain demonstration, that though the Law be the rule according to which *Princes* ought to exercise their authoritie and power, yet the authoritie is not in *Laws*, but in *Persons*; for otherwise why is not a sentence pronounced according to Law by a private person, of as much Authoritie, as a sentence pronounced by a Judge? how does an illegal sentence pronounced by a Judge, come to have any Authoritie? for a sentence contrarie to Law, cannot have the Authoritie of the Law. Why is a legal or illegal sentence reversible, and alterable, when pronounced by one Judge, and irreversible and unalterable, when pronounced by another? For the Law is the same, and the sentence is the same, either according to Law or against it, whoever the Judge be; but it seems the Authoritie of the Persons is not the same, and that makes the difference; so that there is an Authoritie in Persons, in some sence distinct from the Authoritie of Laws, nay superiour to it. For there is such an Authoritie, as, though it cannot

cannot make an illegal act legal, yet, can and often does make an illegal act binding and obligatorie to the Subjects, when pronounced by a competent Judge.

If it be said, that this very authoritie is owing to the law, which appoints Judges and Magistrates to decide controversies, and orders appeals from inferiour to superiour Courts: I would onely ask one short question, Whether the law gives authoritie to any person to judge contrarie to law. If it does not, then all illegal acts are null and void, and lay no obligation on the Subject: and yet this is manifestly false, according to the known Practice of all the known Governments in the world. The most illegal Judgement is valid, till it be reverst by some superiour Power; and the Judgement of the supreme power, though never so illegal, can be repealed by no authoritie but its own. And yet it is absurd to say, that the law gives any man authoritie to Judge contrarie to law: for, to be sure, this is besides the end and intention of the law. Whence then does an illegal act or Judgement derive its authoritie and obligation? the answer is plain, It is from the authoritie of the *Person*, whose act or Judgement it is.

It will be of great use to this controversie, to make this plain and obvious to every understanding; which therefore I shall endeavour to do, as briefly as may be.

1. Then I observe, that there must be a personal power and authoritie antecedent to all civil laws. For there can be no laws without a Law-maker, and there can be no Law-maker, unless there be one or more persons invested with the power of Government, of which making laws is one branch. For a law is nothing else, but the publick and declared will and command of the Law-maker, whether he be the Soveraign *Prince*, or the *People*.

2. And hence it necessarily follows, that a *Soveraign Prince* does not receive his authoritie from the laws, but laws receive their authoritie from him. We are often indeed minded of what BRACTON saies, LEX FACIT REGEM, that the law makes the King; by which that great *Lawyer* was far enough from understanding, that the *King* receives his Soveraign power from the law; for the law has no authoritie,

nor

nor can give any, but what it receives from the *King*; and then it is a wonderful riddle, how the King should receive his authoritie from the law. But when he saies, *The Law makes the King*, he distinguishes a *King* from a *Tyrant*, and his meaning is, that to Govern by laws, makes a *Soveraign Prince* a *King*, as King signifies a Just and equal and beneficial power and authoritie; as appears from the reason he gives for it, *Non est enim Rex, ubi dominatur voluntas, & non lex*; He is no King, who Governs by arbitrarie will, and not by law: not that he is no Soveraign *Prince*, but he is a *Tyrant* and not a *King*.

3. And hence it evidently follows, that the being of Soveraign Power is independent on laws; that is, as a *Soveraign Prince* does not receive his power from the law, so, should he violate the laws by which he is bound to Govern, yet he does not forfeit his power. He breaks his faith to God and to his Countrie, but he is a *Soveraign Prince* still. And this is in effect acknowledged by these men, who so freely confess, that let a *Prince* be what he will, though he trample upon all laws, and exercise an arbitrarie and illegal authoritie, yet his

his person is sacred and inviolable, and irresistible; he must not be touch'd nor opposed. And allow that saying of *David* to be Scripture still, *Who can stretch forth his hand against the Lord's Anointed, and be guiltless?* Now what is it, that makes the person of a King more inviolable and unaccountable than other men? Nothing, that I know of, but his sacred and inviolable authoritie: and therefore it seems, though he act against law, yet he is a *Soveraign Prince*, and the *Lord's Anointed* still ; or else I see no reason, why they might not destroy his person also. And yet if nothing but an inviolable and unaccountable authoritie can make the *Person* of the *King* inviolable and unaccountable, I would gladly know, how it becomes lawful to resist his authoritie, and unlawful to resist his Person. I would desire these men to tell me, whether a *Soveraign Prince* signifies the natural Person, or the Authoritie of a King; and if to divest him of his authoritie, be to kill the *King*, why they may not kill the man too, when they have killed the *King*. Thus when men are forc't to mince Treason and Rebellion, they always speak Nonsense. Those indeed who resist the authorithoritie of their *Prince*, but spare his *Person*, do better than those, who kill him; but those who affirm, that his *Person* is as resistible and accountable as his *Authoritie*, speak more consistently with themselves, and the Principles of Rebellion.

4. And hence I suppose, it plainly appears, that every illegal act the *King* does, is not *an inauthoritative Act*, but laies an obligation on Subjects to yeild, if not an *active*, yet a *passive* obedience. For the *King* receives not his Soveraign Authoritie from the Law, nor does he forfeit his authoritie by breaking the law; and therefore he is a *Soveraign Prince* still; and his most illegal acts, though they have not the authoritie of the law, yet they have the Authoritie of Soveraign Power, which is irresistible and unaccountable.

In a word, it does not become any man who can think three consequences off, to talk of the authoritie of laws in derogation to the authoritie of the Soveraign power. The Soveraign power made the laws, and can repeal them and dispence with them, and make new laws; the onely power and authoritie of the laws is in the power, which can make and execute Laws. Soveraign Power is inseparable from the Person of a Soveraign Prince: and though the exercise of it may be regulated by Laws, and that Prince does very ill, who having consented to such a regulation, breaks the Laws; yet when he acts contrarie to Law, such acts carrie Soveraign and irresistible Authoritie with them, while he continues a Soveraign *Prince.*

But if it be possible to convince all men how vain this pretence of Laws is, to justifie Resistance or Rebellion against a *Prince*, who persecutes without or against Law, I shall only ask two plain questions.

1. Whether the Laws of God and Nature be not as sacred and inviolable as the Laws of our Country? if they be, (and methinks no man should dare say that they are not) why may we not as well resist a *Prince*, who persecutes us against the Laws of God and Nature, as one, who persecutes against the Laws of our Countrey? is not the Prince as much bound to observe the Laws of God and Nature, as the Laws of his Country? if so, then their distinction between suffering with and against Law
signifies

signifies nothing. For all men, who suffer for well-doing, suffer against Law. For by the Laws of God, and the natural ends of humane Government, such men ought to be rewarded, and not punisht. Nay, they suffer contrarie to those Laws, which commanded them to do that good, for which they suffer. Thus the Christians suffered under *Pagan Emperors*, for worshipping one supreme God, and refusing to worship the numerous *Gods* of the *Heathens*; and therefore, according to these principles, might have justified a Rebellion against those unjust and persecuting powers; but the Apostles would not allow this to be a just cause of resistance, as I have already shewn you; and yet I confess I am to seek for the reason of this difference, why we may not resist a *Prince*, who persecutes against the Laws of God, as well as him, who persecutes against the Laws of *England*.

2. My other question is this, Whether a *Prince* have any more authority to make wicked and persecuting Laws, than to persecute without Law? These men *Julian* Apostell us, that if *Paganism* or *Popery* were state established by Law, they were bound to suffer patiently for their Religion, with-

out

out resistance; but since *Christianity* and *Protestancy* is the Religion of the Nation, they are not bound to suffer, but may defend themselves, when they are condemned by no Law. But if we examine this throughly, it is a very weak and trifling Cavil. For what authoritie has a wicked and persecuting Law? and who gave it this authoritie? what authoritie has any Prince to make Laws against the Laws of God? if he have no authoritie, then it is no Law; and then to make a wicked Law to persecute good men, is the same thing, as to persecute without Law, nay as to persecute against Law. The pretence for resistance is, when the Prince persecutes without authority. Now I say, a *Prince* has no more authoritie to make wicked persecuting Laws, than to persecute without Law. Should a *Popish Prince* procure all our good Laws for the *Protestant Religion* to be repealed, and establish *Popery* by Law, and make it death not to be a *Papist*, he would have no more real authoritie to do this, than to persecute *Protestants* without repealing the Laws. A Soverain and unaccountable power will justifie both, so as to make resistance unlawful; but if it cannot justifie

stifie both, it can juftifie neither. For a *Prince* has no more authoritie to make a bad Law, than to break a good one; fo that this principle will lead them a great deal farther than they pretend to; and let the *Laws* of the *Land* be what they will, in time they may come to think it a juft reafon for Rebellion, to pull down *Antichrift*, and to fet up *Chrift Jefus* upon this Throne. This I hope is a fufficient anfwer to the two firft objections, That we are bound by no Law to fuffer againft Law; And that the *Prince* has no authoritie againft Law.

3. The next objection is, that they have a natural right of *felf-prefervation* and *felf-defence* againft unjuft and illegal violence. This very pretence was made great ufe of to wheadle people into this late Confpiracie. Thofe who were employed to prepare and difpofe men for *Rebellion*, askt them, whether they would not defend themfelves, if any man came to cut their throats: this they readily faid they would: when they had gained this point, they askt them, whether they did not value their Liberties, as much as their Lives; and whether they would not defend them alfo. And thus they might have proceeded to any

part

part of their Liberties, if they had pleaſed; for they have the ſame right to any part, as to the whole, and thus ſelf-defence would at laſt reach to the ſmalleſt occaſion of diſcontent or jealouſie, or diſlike of *Publick Government.*

Now in anſwer to this, I readily grant, that every man has a natural right to preſerve and defend his life by all lawful means; but we muſt not think every thing lawful, which we have ſtrength and power and opportunity to do; and therefore to give a full anſwer to this plea, let us conſider,

1. That ſelf-defence was never allowed by God or Nature againſt publick authority, but only againſt private violence. There was a time, when Fathers had the power of life and death over their own Children; now I would only ask theſe men, whether if a Son at that time ſaw his Father coming to kill him, and that as he thought very unjuſtly, he might kill his Father to defend himſelf. This never was allowed by the moſt barbarous Nations in the world; and yet it may be juſtified by this principle of ſelf-defence, as it is urged by thoſe men; which is a plain argument that it is falſe. It is an expreſs Law, that *he that ſmiteth*

teth his Father or his Mother shall be surely put to death, 21 *Exod.* 15. and yet then the power of Parents was restrained by publick Laws. And the authoritie of a Prince is not less sacred than of a Parent; he's God's Minister and Vicegerent, and Subjects are expresly forbid to resist; and it is a vain thing to pretend a natural right against the express Law of God.

2. For the sole power of the Sword is in the King's hands, and therefore no private man can take the Sword in his own defence but by the King's authoritie, and certainly he cannot be presumed to give any man authoritie to use the Sword against himself. And therefore as Christ tells *Peter*, *he that takes the Sword shall perish by the Sword*; he who draws the Sword against the lawful powers, deserves to die by it.

3. We may consider also, that it is an external Law, that private defence must give place to the publick good. Now he that takes Arms to defend his own life and some few others, involves a whole Nation in blood and confusion, and occasions the miserable slaughter of more men, than a long succession of Tyrants could destroy. Such men sacrifice

many

many thousand lives, both of friends and enemies, the happiness and prosperity of many thousand Families, the publick peace and tranquillity of the Nation, to a private self-defence; and if this be the Law of Nature, we may well call Nature a step-mother, that has armed us to our own ruine and confusion.

4. And therefore we may farther observe, that Non-resistance and subjection to government, is the best way for every mans private defence. Our Atheistical Politicians, who know no other Law of nature, but self-defence, make this the Original of humane Societies; That it is a voluntarie combination for self-defence. For this reason they set up Princes and Rulers over them, and put the power of the sword into their hands, that they may administer Justice, and defend their Subjects from publick and private violence: and they are certainly so far in the right, that publick Government is the best securitie not onely of the publick peace, but of every mans private interest; nay it is so, though our Prince be a Tyrant, as I have already shewn you, that no Government can be secure without an irresistible and un-

unaccountable power. So that the natural right of self-defence is so far from justifying Rebellion against Princes, that it absolutely condemns it, as destructive of the best and most effectual means to preserve ourselves: for though by Non-resistance a man may expose his life to the furie of a Tyrant, so he may loose his life in any other way of defence; but publick Government is the best and surest defence, and therefore to resist publick Government, is to destroy the best means of self-defence.

5. However, this principle of self-defence, to be sure, cannot justifie a Rebellion, when men do not suffer any actual violence; and therefore those men who were drawn into this late Conspiracie, when they saw no bodie attempt cutting their throats, when they saw none of their liberties invaded, were so well prepared to be Rebels, that they needed no arguments to perswade them to it.

4. The next objection against the Doctrine of Non-resistance is this, That it destroys the difference between an absolute and limited Monarchy, between a Prince whose will is his Law, and a Prince, who is bound to govern by Law; which undermines the Foundamental

con-

constitution of the English Government. If this were true, I confess, it were a very hard case for the Ministers of the Church of *England*, who must either preach up resistance, contrarie to the Laws of the Gospel, and the sence and practice of the Christian Church in all Ages, or must preach up Non-resistance, to the destruction of the Government under which they live; but thanks be to God, this is not true. For the difference between an absolute and limited Monarchy, is not, that resistance is unlawful in one case, and lawful in another: for a Monarch, the exercise of whose power is limited and regulated by Laws, is as irresistible, as the most absolute Monarch, whose will is his Law; and if he were not, I would venture to say, that the most absolute and Despotick Government, is more for the publick good, than a limited Monarchy.

But the difference lies in this, that an absolute Monarch is under the Government of no Law, but his own will; he can make and repeal Laws at his pleasure, without asking the consent of any of his Subjects; he can impose what Taxes he pleases, and is not tied up to strict Rules and formalities of Law in

the

the Supreme Powers.

the execution of Justice; but it is quite contrarie in a limited Monarchy, where the excercise of Soveraign Power is regulated by known and standing Laws, which the Prince can neither make nor repeal without the consent of the people. No man can loose his Life or Estate without a legal process and Tryal: no Monies can be levyed, nor any Taxes imposed on the Subject, but by Authority of Parliament: which makes the case of Subjects differ very much from those, who live under an Arbitrary Prince.

No, you will say, the case is just the same: for what do Laws signifie, when a Prince must not be resisted, though he break these Laws, and Govern by an Arbitrarie and Lawless will? He may make himself as absolute, as the *Great Turk* or the *Mogul*, whenever he pleases; for what should hinder him, when all men's hands are tied by this Doctrine of Non-resistance? Now it must be acknowledged, that there is a possibilitie for such a Prince to Govern arbitrarily, and to trample upon all laws; and yet the difference between an absolute and limited Monarchy is vastly great.

1. For this Prince, though he may **make** his will a Law to himself, and

the onely rule of his Government, yet he cannot make it the Law of the Land: he may break Laws, but he can neither make nor repeal them; and therefore he can never alter the frame and constitution of the Government, though he may at present interrupt the regular administration of it: and this is a great securitie to posteritie, and a present restraint upon himself.

2. For it is a mightie uneasie thing to any Prince, to govern contrarie to known Laws. He offers as great and constant violence to himself, as he does to his Subjects. He cannot raise mony, nor impose any Taxes without the consent of his Subjects, nor take away any man's life without a legal Tryal (which an absolute Prince may do) but he is guiltie of rapine and murder; and feels the same rebukes in his own mind, for such illegal actions, though his impositions be but reasonable and moderate, and he put no man to death, but who very well deserves it, that an *absolute Tyrant* does for the most barbarous oppressions and cruelties. The breach of his Oath to God, and his promises and engagements to his Subjects, makes the excercise of such an arbitrarie power very trouble-

troublesome: and though his Subjects are bound not to resist, yet his own guilty fears will not suffer him to be secure: and arbitrarie Power is not so luscious a thing, as to tempt men to forfeit all the ease and pleasure, and securitie of Government, for the sake of it.

3. Though Subjects must not resist such a *Prince*, who violates the Laws of his Kingdom; yet they are not bound to obey him, nor to serve him in his usurpations. Subjects are bound to obey an *absolute Monarch*, and to serve his will in lawful things, though they be hard and grievous; but in a *limited Monarchy*, which is governed by Laws, Subjects are bound to yeild an active obedience onely according to Law, though they are bound not to resist, when they suffer against Law. Now it is a mighty uneasy thing to the greatest *Tyrant*, to govern always by force; and no Prince in a limited Monarchy can make himself absolute, unless his own Subjects assist him to do so.

4. And yet it is very dangerous for any Subject to serve his *Prince* contrary to Law. Though the *Prince* himself is unaccountable and irresistible, yet his *Ministers* may be called to an account,

and be punish't for it; and the *Prince* may think fit to look on quietly, and see it done: or if they escape at present, yet it may be time enough to suffer for it under the next *Prince*; which we see by experience makes all men wary how they serve their *Prince* against Law. None but persons of desperate fortunes will do this bare-fac't; and those are not always to be met with, and as seldom fit to be employ'd.

5. And therefore we may observe, that by the fundamental Laws of our Government, as the *Prince* must Govern by Law, so he is irresistible: which shews, that our wise Law-makers did not think, that *Non-resistance* was destructive of a *limited Monarchy*.

6 And in this long succession of *Princes* in this *Kingdom*, there has been no *Prince* that has cast off the Authority of Laws, or usurpt an absolute and arbitrary Power: which shews how vain those fears are, which disturb the fancies and imaginations of Rebels, if they be not pretended onely to disturb the publick Peace.

7. *Non-resistance* is certainly the best way to prevent the change of a *limited* into an *absolute* Monarchy. The Laws of

of *England* have made such an admirable provision for the honour and prosperous Government of the Prince, and the security of the Subject, that the *Kings* of *England* have as little temptation to desire to be absolute, while their *Subjects* are obedient and governable, as their Subjects have, that they should be so. And if ever *our Kings* attempt to make themselves absolute (which thanks be to God, we have no prospect of yet) it will be owing to the factious and traiterous dispositions of Subjects. When Subjects once learn the trade of murdering Princes, and rebelling against them, it is time then for Princes to look to themselves; and if ever our posterity should suffer under so unhappy a change of Government, they will have reason for ever to curse the Fanatick rage and fury of this Age; and the best way to remove that scandal, which has been already given to Princes, is by a publick profession and practice of this great Gospel-duty of Non-resistance.

8. The last objection against Non-resistance is this, that if resistance in no case be allowed, the mischiefs and inconveniences to Mankind may be intolerable. To which I shall briefly return these following answers. 1.

1. That bare Possibilities are no argument against any thing. For that which may be, may not be; and there is nothing in this world, how good or useful or necessary soever it be in its self, but may possibly be attended with very great inconveniences; and if we must reject that which is good and useful in it self, for the sake of some possible inconveniences, which may attend it, we must condemn the very best things. Modesty and Humility, Justice, and Temperance, are great and excellent Vertues: and yet we may live in such an age, when these Vertues shall beggar a man, and expose him to contempt. Mercy and Clemency is a noble quality in a Prince, and yet it is possible, that the Clemency of a Prince may ruine him, and he may spare Traitors Lives, till they take away his. Marriage is a Divine Institution, which contributes as much to the happiness and comfort of humane life, as any one thing in this world; and yet it may be you cannot name any thing neither, which many times proves so great a plague and curse to Mankind. Thus Non-resistance is a great and excellent duty, and absolutely necessary to the peace and order and good

good government of the world; but yet a bad Prince may take the advantage of it, to do a great deal of mischief. And what follows from hence? that Non-resistance is no duty, because it may possibly be attended with evil consequences? then you can hardly name any thing, which is our duty; for the most excellent Vertues may at one time or other expose us to very great inconveniences; but when they do so, we must not deny them to be our duty, because we shall suffer by it; but must bear our sufferings patiently, and expect our reward from God. And yet that there is not so much danger in Non-resistance, as these men would perswade the world, I hope appears from my answers to the last objection.

2. When we talk of inconveniences, we must weigh the inconveniences on both sides, and consider which are greatest. We may suffer great inconveniences by Non-resistance, when our Prince happens to prove a Tyrant; but shall we suffer fewer inconveniences were it lawful for Subjects to resist?

Which is the greatest and most merciless Tyrant? an arbitrary and lawless Prince, or a Civil War? which will destroy

stroy most mens Lives? a *Nero* or *Dioclesian*, or a pitcht Battel? who will devour most Estates? a Covetous and Rapacious Prince, or an insolent Army, and hungry Rabble? which is the greatest oppression of the Subject? some illegal Taxes, or Plunderings, Decimations, and Sequestrations?

Who are most likely to abuse their power? the Prince, or the people? which is most probable, that a Prince should oppress his dutiful and obedient Subjects, or that some factious and designing men should misrepresent the government of their Prince, and that the giddy multitude should believe them? who is most likely to make a change and alteration in government? an Hereditary Prince, or the People, who are fond of innovations?

While Soverain and irresistible power is in the hands of the Prince, it is possible we may sometimes have a good one, and then we shall find no inconvenience in the Doctrine of Non-resistance. Nay, it is possible, we may have a great many good Princes, for one bad one; for Monsters are not so common, as more natural productions: so that the inconveniences we may suffer by this Doctrine

ctrine will but seldom happen; but had the people power to resist, it is almost impossible, that publick government should ever be quiet and secure for half an age together: they are as unstable as the Seas, and as easily moved with every breath, and as outragious and tempestuous too. These are not some guesses and probabilities, but demonstrations in this unhappy age, wherein we have seen all these things acted.

The CONCLUSION,

Containing a short Dissuasive from Resistance and Rebellion.

HAving thus largely proved that Subjection and Non-resistance is a necessary duty, which Subjects owe to Soverain Princes, and answered all those objections which are made against it; the result of all is, to perswade Subjects to the practise of it. And St. *Paul* urges two very powerful arguments to perswade us to it, *Rom.* 13.

1. That *the powers are of God, and he that resisteth the powers, resisteth the ordinance of God.* And certainly he is no Christian who disputes obedience to the Divine Ordinance and Constitution. A Prince is the Image, the Vice-gerent of God, and therefore Princes are called *Gods* in Scripture, and be he what he will, a good or a bad Prince, while God thinks fit to advance him to the Throne, it becomes us to submit and reverence the Divine Authority. Will you

you lift up your hand against God? will you cast off his authority and government too? does not he know how to rule us? how to chuse a Prince for us? The greatest Rebel would blush to say this in so many words, and yet this is the Language of Rebellion. Men dislike their Prince, that is, that Governour, whom God sets over them: they rebel against their Prince, they Depose him, they Murder him; that is, they disown the Authority of God, they deface and destroy his Image, and offer scorn and contempt to his Vice gerent. Earthly Princes look upon every affront and disgrace done to their Ministers and Lieutenants, to be a contempt of their own Authority; and so does God too: he who pulls down a Prince, denies Gods authority to set him up, and affronts his wisdom in chusing him.

2. And therefore such men must not expect to escape a deserved punishment, *they shall receive to themselves damnation.* Now κρίμα. may either signifie the punishment of Rebellion in this world, or in the next; and here it signifies both.

1. They shall be punisht in this world. And whoever consults Ancient and Modern

der Histories, will find, that Rebels very seldom escape punishment in this world. How often does God defeat all their Counsels, discover their secret Plots and Conspiracies! and if they be prosperous for a while, yet vengeance overtakes them: if they escape punishment from men, they are punisht by some such remarkable providence, as bears the Characters of a Divine Justice in it.

2. However, such men shall not escape the punishments of the other world; and if you believe there is a Hell for Rebels and Traitors, the punishment of resistance is infinitely greater than all the mischiefs which can befal you in subjection to Princes, and a patient suffering for well doing. *What shall it profit a man, though he should gain the whole world*, which is something more than a single Crown and Kingdom, *and loose his own Soul?* Though an universal Empire were the reward of Rebellion, such a glorious Traitor, who parts with his Soul for it, would have no great reason to boast much of his purchase. Let us then reverence the Divine Judgments, let us patiently submit to our King, though he should persecute and oppress us; and expect our protection here from the

the Divine Providence, and our reward in Heaven; which is the fame encouragement to Non-refiftance, which we have to the practife of any other Vertue. Were the advantages and difadvantages of Refiftance and Non-refiftance in this world fairly eftimated, it were much more eligible to fubmit, than to rebel againft our Prince; but there can be no comparifon between thefe two, when we take the other world into the account. The laft Judgment weighs down all other confiderations; and certainly Rebellion may well be faid to be as the fin of Witchcraft, when it fo inchants men, that they are refolved to be Rebels, though they be damned for it.

THE END.

BOOKS Printed for *Fincham Gardiner*.

1. A Perswasive to Communion with the Church of *England*.
2. A Resolution of some Cases of Conscience which respect Church-Communion.
3. The Case of Indifferent things used in the Worship of God, proposed and Stated, by considering these Questions, &c.
4. A Discourse about Edification.
5. The Resolution of this Case of Conscience, *Whether the Church of* Englands *Symbolizing so far as it doth with the Church of* Rome, *makes it unlawful to hold Communion with the Church of* England?
6. A Letter to *Anonymus*, in answer to his three Letters to Dr. *Sherlock* about Church-Communion.
7. Certain Cases of Conscience resolved, concerning the Lawfulness of joyning with Forms of Prayer in Publick Worship. In two Parts.
8. The Case of mixt Communion: Whether it be Lawful to Separate from

Books Printed for F. Gardiner.

a Church upon the account of promiscuous Congregations and mixt Communions?

9. An Answer to the Dissenters Objections against the Common Prayers, and some other parts of Divine Service prescribed in the Liturgy of the Church of *England*.

10. The Case of Kneeling at the Holy Sacrament stated and resolved, &c. In two Parts.

11. A Discourse of Profiting by Sermons, and of going to hear where men think they can profit most.

12. A serious Exhortation, with some important Advices, relating to the late Cases about Conformity, recommended to the present Dissenters from the Church of *England*.

13. An Argument for Union; taken from the true interest of those Dissenters in *England* who profess and call themselves Protestants.

14. Some Considerations about the Case of Scandal, or giving Offence to Weak Brethren.

15. The Case of Infant-Baptism, in Five Questions, &c.

16. The Charge of Scandal, and giving Offence by Conformity, Refelled,

and

Books Printed for F. Gardiner.

and Reflected back upon Separation, &c.

1. A Discourse about the charge of Novelty upon the Reformed Church of *England*, made by the Papists asking of us the Question, Where was our Religion before *Luther*?

2. A Discourse about Tradition, shewing what is meant by it, and what Tradition is to be received, and what Tradition is to be rejected.

3. The difference of the Case between the Separation of Protestants from the Church of *Rome*, and the Separation of Dissenters from the Church of *England*.

4. The Protestant Resolution of Faith, &c.

Some Seasonable Reflections on the Discovery of the late Plot, being a Sermon preached on that occasion, by *W. Sherlock*, D. D. Rector of St. *George Buttolph-lane, London*.

King *David's* Deliverance: or, the Conspiracy of *Absolon* and *Achitophel* defeated, in a Sermon Preached on the day of Thanksgiving appointed for the Discovery of the late Fanatical Plot. By *Thomas Long*, B. D. one of the Prebendaries of *Exon*.